D0178719

VERONICA GUERIN

THE LIFE AND DEATH OF A
CRIME REPORTER

Emily O'Reilly worked as a political columnist at the *Sunday Times* and as the Political Editor of the *Sunday Business Post*. A former Nieman Fellow at Harvard University, she has been Journalist of the Year and Woman Journalist of the Year. In 2003 she was appointed as Ireland's first woman Ombudsman and Freedom of Information Commissioner. She is the author of two books; *Candidate: The Truth Behind the Presidential Campaign* (1991), and *Masterminds of the Right* (1992). Emily O'Reilly lives in Howth, County Dublin, with her husband Stephen Ryan and their five children.

WITHDRAWN

BY EMILY O'REILLY

Candidate: The Truth Behind the Presidential Campaign
Masterminds of the Right
Veronica Guerin: The Life and Death of a Crime Reporter

WITHDRAWN

Emily O'Reilly

VERONICA GUERIN

THE LIFE AND DEATH
OF A CRIME REPORTER

V

VINTAGE

Published by Vintage 1998

6 8 10 9 7 5

Copyright © Emily O'Reilly 1998

Emily O'Reilly has asserted her right under the Copyright, Designs and Patents Act 1988 to be identified as the author of this work

This book is sold subject to the condition that it shall not, by way of trade or otherwise, be lent, resold, hired out, or otherwise circulated without the publisher's prior consent in any form of binding or cover other than that in which it is published and without a similar condition, including this condition, being imposed on the subsequent purchaser

Vintage
Random House, 20 Vauxhall Bridge Road, London SW1V 2SA
Random House Australia (Pty) Limited
20 Alfred Street, Milsons Point, Sydney,
New South Wales 2061, Australia

Random House New Zealand Limited
18 Poland Road, Glenfield,
Auckland 10, New Zealand

Random House South Africa (Pty) Limited
Endulini, 5a Jubilee Road, Parktown 2193, South Africa

Random House UK Limited Reg. No. 954009

A CIP catalogue record for this book
is available from the British Library

ISBN 0 09 976151 3

Papers used by Random House UK Limited are natural, recyclable products made from wood grown in sustainable forests. The manufacturing processes conform to the environmental regulations of the country of origin

Set in 10½/12 Sabon by SX Composing DTP, Rayleigh, Essex
Printed and bound in Great Britain by
Cox & Wyman Ltd, Reading, Berkshire

A VINTAGE ORIGINAL

For the late, great Howard Simons once again

Contents

ACKNOWLEDGEMENTS

My love and thanks as ever to Stephen. To Jessica, Daniel, Zoe and Holly for being there. To Ann for being there with them. To Jonathan Williams for his endeavours on my behalf. To everyone who was courageous enough to contribute openly to this book and especially Veronica's brother Jimmy Guerin. To Sarah Binchy, Cora Ennis and Damien Corless for research.

And to 'Oscar' for what was and what might have been.

Chronology

1990	Veronica Guerin begins her career in journalism with the *Sunday Business Post*.
1993	Moves to the *Sunday Tribune* in January.
1994	Begins work with the *Sunday Independent*, specialising in crime reporting. Her first article for the newspaper is published on January 9.
October 7 1994	Shots are fired through the window of her home into an empty room.
January 30 1995	Veronica is shot in the leg in the hallway of her home. She reportedly tells colleagues that she believes that this was an attempt on her life.
September 1995	Veronica is assaulted by John Gilligan, the self-confessed 'chief suspect' in her murder.
June 26 1996	Veronica is shot dead in her car on the outskirts of Dublin.

Principals

Veronica Guerin	37-year-old Dublin-born journalist.
Graham Turley	Veronica's husband.
Cathal Turley	Veronica and Graham's son; six years of age when Veronica was shot.
Jimmy, Marie-Therese, Martin, Clare Guerin	Veronica's siblings.
Bernadette Guerin	Veronica's widowed mother.
Dr A.J.F. (Tony) O'Reilly	Chairman of Independent Newspapers. Chairman of Heinz Corporation.
David Palmer	Managing Director of Independent Newspapers (Ireland)
Aengus Fanning	Editor of *Sunday Independent*.
Anne Harris	Deputy Editor of the *Sunday Independent*
Willie Kealy	News Editor of *Sunday Independent*.
Paddy Prendiville	Editor of *Phoenix* magazine and a close friend of Veronica.
Damien Kiberd	Editor of *Sunday Business Post*.
Vincent Browne	Former editor of *Sunday Tribune*.
Rory Godson	Former business editor of *Sunday Tribune*; now Irish editor of *Sunday Times*.

Alan Byrne	Former news editor of *Sunday Tribune*.
John Traynor	One of Veronica's key criminal contacts.
John Gilligan	'Chief suspect' in Veronica Guerin's murder; had allegedly beaten her up a short time before her death.

INTRODUCTION

'Most newspapers might see journalism as a higher calling and the market may be incidental. I think we live or die by the market.'

Aengus Fanning, editor, *Sunday Independent*, interviewed by Ivor Kenny in *Talking to Ourselves*, published by Kenny's Book Shop and Art Gallery, 1994.

By the time I began to write this book – almost a full year after her death – tens of thousands of words had been written about Veronica Guerin, mostly by the newspaper in whose employ she died, the *Sunday Independent*.

From time to time, the newspaper had published pieces apparently written by Graham Turley, Veronica's husband. Graham and his lawyers had also been involved in negotiations with at least one film company over the rights to screen a version of Veronica's life story. Several documentaries, in Ireland, Britain and the United States, had already been screened.

The publisher's early publicity 'blurb' had suggested that this book would not promote the official line on Veronica's career and Veronica's death.

Clearly, the *Sunday Independent* found such a degree of independence worrying, and it made that known. In June 1997, the proposed book began to draw fire from the O'Reilly stable – those sections of the Irish media owned or controlled by the Independent Group.

The *Sunday Tribune* quoted Veronica's husband, on Sunday June 22, as being 'disgusted' by the move to publish the book.

On RTE's radio one, presenter Andy O'Mahony had invited publisher Anne O'Donnell and *Sunday Independent* writer Patricia Redlich to review that day's papers – a regular item on O'Mahony's popular programme 'The Sunday Show'.

O'Mahony mentioned the Guerin book story and Redlich became extremely angry. She suggested that the working title of the book, *Dying for the Market*, was 'obscene', disputing that anyone, bar the people who had organised and executed Veronica's murder, held any responsibility for her death.

Everything we needed to know about Veronica's death, she insisted, was already in the public domain. It was a classic *Sunday Independent* attack on an 'enemy' – over the top, as personally offensive as possible, serving, knowingly or unknowingly, the protection of the corporate interests of O'Reilly's media stronghold.

O'Donnell's contribution was more muted, but similarly odd. She said that she was a publisher, but she would not publish such a book against the wishes of Veronica Guerin's family.

The following day it was the turn of the *Irish Sun* and the *Irish Mirror* to attack the idea. In the *Mirror*, tucked beside a shot of a *Baywatch* actress, was a plagiarised version of the *Tribune* story. The *Sun* ran the same plagiarised version, as well as an editorial on the *Sunday Tribune*'s contrived 'controversy' under the heading 'Book of Shame'.

It read: 'It happened exactly one year ago this Thursday. Investigative journalist Veronica Guerin was shot dead in her car. Her heartbroken husband Graham says this anniversary month has been most distressing. How cruel then, for publishers to defy the family's express wishes and rush out a book.'

The editorial went on to say that, by suggesting that Veronica Guerin's actions were reckless, her 'courageous crusade against Dublin crime' was 'cheapened by jibes about the dubious ethics of modern journalism'.

It concluded with the warning that I, the author, was unconnected to the Guerin family. In the light of that, the public were exhorted to honour Veronica's memory by refusing to buy the book.

Why did the news that this book was to be published excite such a strong reaction?

Could it be that they suspected that this book would present a version of Veronica's life over which neither Graham Turley nor the *Sunday Independent* could exercise control?

The *Sunday Independent* had been acting as part agent, part filtering system for Graham. Many journalists and producers found themselves directed to the paper's news editor, Willie Kealy, when they looked for access to Veronica's husband.

This was done primarily to protect Graham, but there may have been a further agenda. Some people felt that the *Sunday Independent* had a lot of questions to answer about its own responsibility in relation to Veronica Guerin. It needed to exercise as much media management as possible. It could oversee the output of its own vast Independent stable, but the few journalists outside the Independent were a different matter.

Later that day I came across a one-page statement that had lain for some months on my mantelpiece. It was headed 'The Guerin Principles'. This was a set of media standards published by journalist groups and newspaper editors after Veronica's death. The last Guerin principle read: 'Media workers resolve to resist any attempts at intimidation in whatever form and from whatever quarter.'

I also recalled the television advertisement that the *Sunday Independent* had run some days after her death. It featured a black and white photograph of Veronica; underneath were printed her dates of birth and death. The caption read: 'News is something that someone, somewhere, doesn't want published.'

It seemed now that just one year after her death, a lot of

journalists and newspapers had already forgotten the fine words they had spoken at the time. It also seemed that the story I was about to tell very definitely qualified as news.

I

A JOURNALIST DIES

One truth at least did not change in the weeks and months that followed Veronica Guerin's murder. Everybody remembered where they were when they heard the news.

It was lunchtime on June 26 1996. I was sitting in the self-service restaurant of Leinster House, the Kildare Street, Dublin, building that houses the Dáil[1] and Seanad Eireann.[2] It was a middle table; I had my back to the door, and was chatting away about nothing in particular to a colleague, a journalist with the *Sunday Independent*, John Drennan, idling away an hour until Taoiseach's Question Time later that afternoon.[3]

Fianna Fáil's press secretary, Michael Ronayne, stopped at our table to talk. A Fianna Fáil TD,[4] Seán Doherty, had said earlier that morning that he would vote against the impending divorce legislation if a vote were called. We speculated on its significance. We concluded that it had none.

Another party press officer, Mandy Johnson, approached Ronayne and whispered something before moving away. Ronayne said there was a rumour that Veronica Guerin, crime correspondent on the *Sunday Independent* had been shot again. He was going to ring RTE, Ireland's state broadcasting network, he said, and find out if it was true.

Ronayne left. Drennan and I looked at each other. I think I

1 Parliament.
2 Senate.
3 The Taoiseach is the Irish Prime Minister.
4 Teachta Dala, member of parliament.

grinned in that irrational way you do when someone tells you bad news. I told John that I would go after Ronayne and that if I heard anything I would come back and tell him.

I went outside. Ronayne was sitting on a large leather armchair in the corridor folding down the handset on his mobile. He looked up as I approached. He said some words that I cannot now remember and then he said, 'She's dead.'

It was 1.25 p.m. Veronica had been lying dead in her car on a dual carriageway on the outskirts of Dublin for just over twenty minutes. Graham Turley, her husband, would not be told of her death until shortly after 2 p.m. In retrospect, it seemed wrong, invasive, that we should know before him.

As Ronayne and I stood there, a door to our left opened. In brisk procession, looking forward to their lunch, out came the Taoiseach, John Bruton, the Tánaiste,[5] Dick Spring, a slew of cabinet ministers and TDs in their wake.

A vote in the chamber had just ended. We told them what we had heard. Bruton and Spring already knew; a message had been passed to them inside the chamber. The news rippled back through the rows of emerging TDs. For a while everyone just stood there, awkwardly, then moved away.

At this stage the report was technically unconfirmed. The lunchtime radio news on Ireland's radio one carried a report that a woman had been shot dead on the Naas dual carriageway. Privately, the Gardaí[6] were telling the press that it was Veronica. Her red Opel Calibra car and its number plates were well known to themselves and criminals.

I went back into the restaurant and told John Drennan that Veronica was dead. I walked upstairs to my office in the political correspondents' room on the second floor of Leinster House. Already some of them had started working on the story.

The lunchtime news programme was just ending. Later I learnt that a fax had come through to the producer. It was from the *Evening Herald*, a sister paper of the *Sunday*

5 Deputy Prime Minister.
6 Irish police force.

Independent. The fax contained the *Herald*'s latest headline: 'Veronica Guerin is Shot Dead.'

It was a feature of the lunchtime programme to read out the early evening paper headlines, but Veronica had been dead for less than three-quarters of an hour. She had not been formally identified. Nobody knew whether her family had been contacted or not. The producer put the fax to one side.

I sat at my desk and rang Paddy Prendiville, the editor of *Phoenix* magazine, a good friend of mine but an even closer friend of Veronica's. Paddy wasn't there; he was out on sick leave, so I called his home. He had heard the news just five minutes earlier. His voice was agitated, excited from the shock, railing about those whom he believed had murdered one of his closest friends. He said he was trying to contact some of Veronica's family.

Bits and pieces of news began trickling in to Leinster House. Colleagues were talking to their news desks and their friends, trading information. At first the story was fuzzy, confused. Someone said it was a set-up, that Veronica had gone to meet a contact at the Green Isle Hotel that borders the carriageway. She had gone there and had been shot.

Someone else had spoken to a male friend of Veronica, who claimed that she had been terrified for weeks, scared that her life was in danger, worried about one particular individual, an alleged drug dealer, who had threatened her. The friend had said that he had never known her to be so concerned. None of the names meant anything to me nor to most people in that building on that day.

That afternoon I had nothing to do. I would not have to write about this for another two days, so I just drifted about Leinster House. At half-past four I went to the Dáil bar and had a drink. TDs came and commiserated with me and other journalists on the death of a colleague. But hardly any of my colleagues there that afternoon had known her. Even some of those who were working on the *Sunday Independent* had never met her. For them she was just a story they had read about when she was shot at the first time, the second time and now this final time. She was not a colleague of whom they necessarily had any memories, or with whom they had shared journalistic experiences.

Journalists are, to some extent, a community, but Veronica had been a latecomer to journalism; she had no history. She also worked almost entirely alone.

I had known Veronica Guerin for eleven years, our relationship had always been friendly, but it would be unrealistic to describe us as close. I had met her first in 1985 when she was working as a part-researcher, part-public relations consultant for Fianna Fáil.

In 1986 I got engaged and Veronica met me and gave me a bottle of champagne. We met up sporadically over the next ten years. On the last occasion we had met, about three months before she died, I had given her flowers, belated congratulations for a journalism award she had received. Later we walked back to her car, the red Opel in which she would one day die, and she left me at the gate of Leinster House.

In the years that followed our first meeting, I had noted her career path, her stories. Before and after her death, Paddy Prendiville filled me in on other aspects of her life. I had never met her husband or her child, never been in her house. But we still had a lot in common. We were about the same age; she was a year or two younger. We were both mothers and we had the shared experience of women in high-profile positions in the media.

Later I realised that I didn't know her at all. Neither did most of the people she had befriended during her six years as a journalist.

At four o'clock on the afternoon she died, a fat bundle of the *Evening Herald* was placed beside the cash desk in the restaurant in Leinster House. The headline read: 'Veronica Guerin is Shot Dead.' In its simplicity it was devastating.

At half-past four, tributes were paid to Veronica by the Taoiseach and the party leaders in the Dáil chamber. I sat in the press gallery. The journalistic part of my brain detached itself and paid attention. The rest of me was floating in some other mental space.

The Taoiseach talked about press freedom and praised its

role in our democracy. It was a rather novel view from a man whose leadership style was perceived as being defined by media paranoia, by an overriding imperative to keep information about his administration away from the press.

Mary Harney, the leader of the Progressive Democrats, stood and said that Veronica had been shot twice in the face and three times in the chest. Afterwards, somebody said that the detailing of her murder in that way was gratuitous.

I learnt later that Veronica's face had been unmarked. All the bullets had lodged in her upper body – below the neck. But Harney's description gave me nightmares; I worried about how the undertakers could make her whole again, make her presentable to her husband and her child. I thought about the police and others who had to view her body in the car. I heard that her colleague, crime correspondent Paul Williams, had become physically sick on the Naas Road when he went to view the scene.

The rest of the evening passed in a haze. At five o'clock I listened to a radio interview with her editor, Aengus Fanning. He was shocked, he said, devastated. He had never met a journalist with Veronica's drive, with her sense of 'mission'. He denied that there was anything he could have done to have stopped her pursuing the stories she did.

Even though there had been shots fired through her window. Even though she had been shot in the leg. Even though she had been beaten up. Even though her young son had been threatened with rape, kidnap and murder.

In a newspaper exceptionally well staffed with editors and line managers, supported by legal, public relations and other ancillary advisers, and with the financial might of the O'Reilly media empire behind it, Veronica alone had controlled her destiny.

That was the *Sunday Independent* line then; it remains the *Sunday Independent* line to this day. I later discovered that many people who had worked very closely with Veronica in other newspapers shared Fanning's view. Veronica was, and was permitted to be, a law unto herself.

I did not leave Leinster House until after six o'clock, even though I had no work to do there. Because hardly anybody there knew Veronica, I could not talk to anybody about her.

The next two days passed in a similar, Veronica-saturated, media haze. I read most of the pieces in the papers, heard most of the news bulletins and tributes. My local butcher sympathised with me. My next-door neighbour gave me a hug. A stranger came up in the bank and said, 'Aren't you lucky you only write about business?'

On Thursday morning, the day after her death, RTE radio presenter Joe Duffy read out a listener's suggestion that flowers in memory of Veronica should be placed outside Leinster House. This would be a beautiful, midsummer reminder of her, and its location a reminder to those whom the caller judged to be partially responsible for her death.

Shortly after lunchtime on that day, I walked out past the Leinster House gate, towards Molesworth Street. There, lying against the railings, were four bundles of flowers. When I came back less than an hour later, the number had grown. By teatime, the bank of floral tributes stretched the length of the railing.

Some were garden flowers wrapped in plastic, others Interflora-delivered bouquets. Two were dedicated to Orla Guerin, Veronica's journalistic namesake who, in 1994, had run for election to the European Parliament on the Labour party ticket. Her name was frequently confused with that of the crime reporter. Veronica would have been amused.

Aengus Fanning was interviewed again. Once more he was asked if there was anything he could have done to prevent her death. In that interview, as in others, it was stated, and accepted as part of the public articulation of Veronica's death, that there was nothing he or his newspaper could have done.

She had requested that Gardaí protection be removed in the wake of two earlier attacks. The public had to understand: this was a woman – a journalist – apart; a woman with a mission, someone that no one and no organisation could deflect. The paper, its editor, its management and its owner should not be held to blame.

That day, Aengus Fanning wrote his own tribute to

Veronica Guerin in the editorial page of his sister paper, the *Irish Independent*. It was appropriately sombre and in touch with the country's mood, but it was curiously detached in tone and content. It could have been written by anyone; by the editor of another paper perhaps, by someone who barely knew her.

Most notable was the apparent absence of self-blame, even self-doubt on the part of Fanning. There were constant references to the solitary nature of her work, to her own detachment from the 'normal' workings of, and relationships with, a newspaper. There was absolute acceptance on Fanning's part that nothing and nobody could have stopped her from doing what she did.

Throughout this period, *Independent* editorial and management executives were being advised by the Independent group's corporate public relations consultant, Jim Milton.

Fanning wrote:

This is Irish journalism's darkest day. For the first time, a journalist has been murdered for daring to write about our criminal underworld and daring to chronicle the lives of the brutal people who inhabit it.

It is a blatant and terrifying attack on a free press and on freedom of speech, freedoms which we take too often for granted.

As the Taoiseach, the Tánaiste and the Opposition leaders said yesterday, the murder of our colleague Veronica Guerin is nothing less than an attack on democracy.

If newspapers, television, radio and other media were to be deterred from doing their duty in the public interest by threats, intimidation and murder, it would indeed be time to draw down the blinds on our democracy.

But this, I am convinced, is not going to happen. Veronica Guerin is irreplaceable, to her family, to her colleagues, to Irish journalism, to Independent Newspapers and to the *Sunday Independent*, but I believe her brilliant, short career will be an inspiration to thousands of others all over the world, and that the ruthless forces in society who care nothing for life and liberty will be routed in time.

Veronica Guerin's calm courage was of an entirely different order from that of thousands of journalists in war zones from Belfast to Beirut.

For a start, she always worked on her own, tenuously linked with news desk, family and friends by her mobile phone.

It was the sheer solitariness of her chosen method of work, seven days a week, 52 weeks a year, that marked her out from others.

Not for her the camaraderie of reporters sharing risks and the reward of the story. Veronica, self-deprecating, attractive, wryly humorous, was entirely on her own. She was armed only with her pen, her notebook and her courage when she confronted some of our most dangerous criminals, when she probed into the darkest corners of our underworld and came back with an unending stream of exclusive stories.

It struck me more than once that her bravery was of the type that drove isolated French Resistance fighters to take on the brutal, terrifying power of Nazi Germany, working alone without the comradeship and support of colleagues-in-arms.

I and some of her close colleagues often analysed her work and concluded that the only way she was able to carry on was by calmly facing the fact that she might at some time pay for her courage and her convictions with her life.

But to talk to her about the risks she was taking was unrewarding. She made little of them, and never showed the slightest fear, though I know she was frightened at times. 'Don't be daft,' was a typical reaction when the question of danger to her life was raised.

But she knew, deep in her heart, that her work was always going to be dangerous, that nobody but she could do it, that she had to do it alone, and that without the freedom to move about, it would not be possible.

After the gun attack on her home early last year, the most

comprehensive security precautions were put in place on the north County Dublin home she shared with her husband Graham and son Cathal, who is due to start school next September.

For a time after that, she was under 24-hour Garda protection but she found this irksome. She knew that to do her work effectively she needed the liberty to move freely and quickly. If she didn't have this freedom, I am certain she would have given up journalism.

It was no more than her democratic right and she insisted upon it, but she has paid a terrible price, as have her family and her colleagues.

On Friday I had to write my piece for the *Sunday Business Post*. I thought about writing a 'The-Veronica-I-knew' piece but decided that I was too far down the queue.

Instead I called on the Justice Minister, Nora Owen, to resign. She did not take her cue and rush to hand in her notice but picking on her had assuaged my need to hit out at someone. At this stage, the criminals were just anonymous men, their identities barely hinted at in newspaper articles that had been thoroughly vetted by the lawyers before publication.

At this stage also, I knew little about Veronica's work or how she had gone about it. At this stage, I was making black and white judgements about everybody out of ignorance.

I had rarely read what she wrote, because I didn't take a great interest in crime. I just assumed that, in an increasingly prosperous and increasingly secular country, crime would flourish. I assumed that there were a lot of people cashing in on the 'Celtic tiger' through criminal means. As an area of journalistic or intellectual interest, crime did not excite me. My lack of interest was no aspersion on Veronica or on the quality of her journalism; it was simply a reflection on myself.

I did something else that Friday afternoon. I wrote a short letter to Aengus Fanning and to his deputy Anne Harris. I commiserated with them on Veronica's death and told them that she had often spoken highly and fondly of them. This was not entirely true. On the last few occasions we had met,

Veronica had scarcely spoken a word about either. She was professionally neutral about both. Besides, she hardly ever saw them, though she appeared to be closer to Anne Harris than to Aengus Fanning.

But I wrote this letter because I was thinking about what must be going through their minds at that time. I imagined that they must be feeling guilty in some private way and I wanted to comfort them and say that they should feel OK about their relationship with Veronica. I sent the letter by courier.

Months later Aengus Fanning wrote back. He said the letter had meant more to them than any other that they had received. I found that curious; I also found it unsettling, because by now little seeds of doubt had been sown in my brain about the *Independent*'s behaviour towards its journalist. Later, much later, little seeds of doubt would be sown in my brain about Veronica herself.

Days passed. Veronica was buried in a graveyard close to her home. The nation mourned. Discussion of her death deepened and widened, but not in the mainstream media. There seemed to be separate, public and private, views on the nature of, and reasons for, her death. In public, the picture was of a brave young woman, a mother, fearless, willing to risk her own life in the pursuit of truth, impervious to pressure to quit, the brightest and the best.

In private, though, other questions were raised, about Veronica, her motivation, the level of risk any journalist is justified in taking, her methodology, and – very much in private – the way the *Sunday Independent* had handled her death, the way the *Sunday Independent* had managed Veronica in the two and a half years she had worked there.

When I started this book, the latter issue was my focus. Some months on, the book I began to write had changed. Veronica's story, I had discovered, was as grey as the skies under which she now lies.

2

WHO WAS VERONICA?

'I would, and do, take risks. I would meet anyone, go anywhere for a story.'

Veronica Guerin

Who was Veronica? This was a question often asked in the
days that followed her death. Veronica Guerin was in her
early thirties when she began her career as a journalist. Few of
her journalist colleagues appeared to know what she had
done before that. Veronica was vague when she was asked to
fill in the blanks.

Even her *Sunday Independent* colleagues barely knew her.
Many had never even met her. She worked alone, she did not
have a desk in the Middle Abbey Street building, her work
was conducted from the front seat of her car or in various
rendezvous around Dublin and often outside the capital and
abroad.

Veronica Guerin's life was pieced together in numerous
profiles after her death. In hindsight they were remarkable for
the absence of any substantial detail on her life before entering journalism in 1990, at the age of thirty-two.

In the huge volume of articles written about her since her
death, there is scant detail on the years prior to 1990. The
primary source for autobiographical detail is her husband
Graham Turley. In the handful of interviews he has
given since her death, he makes only fleeting reference to that
time.

Her friend Lise Hand – a woman often described as

Veronica's 'best' friend – gave several interviews, yet she had known Veronica for just three years.

Her longest-standing journalistic friendship was with Paddy Prendiville, the editor of *Phoenix* magazine. He had known her for fourteen years, but admits that he knows very little about her early working life.

Another close friend and colleague, Alan Byrne, said much the same. He found out that she had worked in public relations only when he read about it after her death.

Veronica herself was publicly evasive about her life before she entered journalism. A profile in *Image* magazine in 1994, shortly after she had joined the *Sunday Independent*, stated: 'Educated by the Holy Faith nuns in Killester, she is evasive about what came next. With a wave of her hand, she mentions as previous jobs accountancy, marketing and PR. She has worked as an aide to Charles Haughey and is said to be close to the Haughey family, which would explain her seemingly inexhaustible list of contacts.'

It was the final two paragraphs of the profile that were the most revealing:

She is blessed, she says, with a partner who does not care what hours she works, as long as she is happy and, to compensate for her odd working hours, she will often take her four-year-old son on assignments.

I don't always get home for bedtime. I say I will spend Saturday and Sunday at home and never do. I would get up in the morning and fly anywhere in the world for a story. I would, and do, take risks. I would meet anyone, do anything to get a story. I'm a news hound. There are great opportunities out there for hungry news hounds – and I am hungry.

Some of her friends believed that her reluctance to talk about her earlier life stemmed from embarrassment. Past involvement in public relations clashed with her new image as a tough, investigative reporter.

But the truth was somewhat different. Veronica Guerin did

not want to talk about the past because there was a great deal in her past that she wanted kept out of the public gaze.

The business of ascertaining the full truth about her life is like chasing mercury. Even the reported date of her birth is inaccurate. Every account of Veronica's life published to date has stated that she was born on July 5 1959. It is printed on her gravestone. Yet according to the Register of Births, she was born one year earlier, in 1958. Even allowing for the not-unusual tendency of people – and particularly women – to shave a few years off their age, it seems curious that the error would follow her to her grave.

Veronica's brother Jimmy Guerin, a year or so younger than her, has told the author that the confusion over Veronica's actual date of birth stems from the time the two of them were members of Ógra Fianna Fáil – the youth section of the party. When the pair became too old to qualify for membership, they shaved a number of years off their ages.

Veronica Guerin's childhood was described in profiles after her death as normal, even banal. She was born into a family of five children in the settled, working-class community of Artane in Dublin's northside. Her father, Christopher Guerin, had an accountancy firm, Guerin and Reid, in Gardiner Street. Jimmy Guerin says that his father was one of the few people who really knew Veronica.

At school she was a tomboy, fearless, domineering at times over weaker girls, excelling in sport. She played basketball and soccer, rising to represent Ireland in each. Her approach was intensely physical; she suffered breaks and sprains but none so serious that she gave up.

School and team photographs from the time show a pretty, broad-smiling, young girl. In a tribute published after her death, one friend recalled how once, when playing on the street with friends, a neighbour had taken away their football. He was fed up with the constant stream of children coming into his back garden to retrieve it. No one wanted to go and ask for it back, apart from Veronica. She marched to the door, knocked, politely asked for the ball's return and walked back in triumph some moments later, ball tucked underneath her arm.

The anecdote was remembered and recounted by the friend some weeks after Veronica died. It had an extra resonance then.

The other hallmarks of the woman as a young girl were her charm, her kindness. According to those who remembered her from that time, she was always the one who welcomed in the newcomers to the sports clubs, the one who broke the ice. She became a volunteer worker at the local youth club, organising trips for the poorer children of her parish. She liked people, was fascinated by them even, enjoyed hearing the details of their lives.

The latter characteristic was mentioned by a number of people interviewed for this book. Veronica Guerin had a gift for intimacy; she could draw someone in within minutes of meeting them and in a very short time would know many of the most private details of their life. It was a 'gift' she used to great effect in the many activities in which she became involved in her adult life.

While researching this book, I was struck by the number of people who genuinely believed themselves to be very close to Veronica Guerin. She had more than one best friend, but not a single one who really knew her. What they all shared was a genuine liking for her.

Her closest sibling was Jimmy. He certainly knew his sister very well. Many of the things I subsequently discovered about her earlier life, he knew already.

'We hung around together,' he told me. 'I don't remember *not* knocking around with Veronica. My earliest memories of her are maybe eight or nine years of age when we were going out in crowds. We always went together and there would be fellas and girls knocking around together. We did until the time we left school and then after that we joined Fianna Fáil together.'

Veronica was a supportive and protective sister. She fixed Jimmy up with his first girlfriend. She helped him with his school work.

I was very close to her, I mean I enjoyed her company because she was very good fun. There was only a year between us which is really nothing, so we were more friends than say, ordinary siblings.

I remember going to discos . . . she'd go into town on a Saturday and she'd come home with your gear and this was what you had to wear and she'd have you looking cool. She was always looking out for you in that way.

Veronica was, he says, a real tomboy, and seemed to prefer the company of boys to her female peers. Even when they started to show an interest in the opposite sex, they remained close friends.

The first steady relationship she had went on for eight years, right up until she was, I suppose, twenty, twenty-one, twenty-three, around that. Five of us lads knocked around together and Niall [her boyfriend] was one of them, so by virtue of that relationship, we stayed in the same crowd. And then I'd be going out with a friend of Veronica's. I never regarded her as a sister when we were out, but . . . you'd always look out for her, or her for you . . . just a natural thing.

Jimmy recalls his sister's chief passion as being sport. 'Sport, sport, sport. I mean, not even music. She always loved sport.'

At school, he says, she was academically bright, but lazy. 'She didn't concentrate, she didn't apply herself to school . . . none of us did, but she was a lot brighter than me. She would have been one of the brightest at home.'

The other passion they shared was politics. In their teens, Veronica and Jimmy Guerin became friends with the sons of the former Fianna Fáil leader and Taoiseach Charles J. Haughey. The Guerins were often invited to Haughey's mansion, Abbeville, at Kinsealy in north County Dublin.

Graham Turley, also knew the Haugheys and the couple had met in 1982 through their involvement with Fianna Fáil.

Turley was best man at Haughey's son Ciaran's wedding. He had met Ciaran Haughey when they were both members of the Sea Scouts in Malahide, north County Dublin.

Veronica and Graham called their son Cathal, after Charles Haughey. Veronica used to refer to Haughey himself by the Irish version of his name. Haughey was a guest at their remarkably lavish wedding in 1985 and the couple spent part of their honeymoon on his island home off the Kerry coast, Inishvickillaune.

Veronica Guerin first became involved in Fianna Fáil in the mid-to-late seventies, as part of a group of other young people active in Haughey's constituency in north Dublin.

A party colleague from that time remembers that the group emerged from a school gang into Ogra Fianna Fáil. They were passionate supporters of Haughey and of the more republican wing of the party. They liked to express their nationalism by sprinkling their conversations with short bursts of Irish.

Of Veronica, the party colleague recalls: 'She was very much into Haughey and the whole social life. She loved hanging around Abbeville.' And the attraction between the young political activist and the about-to-be leader of Fianna Fáil was mutual. Haughey became very fond of Veronica. He liked her spirit, her humour, her energy – most of all he liked her adoration. Some years later, he recounted with pride and affection how Veronica had discharged herself from hospital in order to take part in a demonstration in support of him during one of the several 'heaves' against his leadership in the early 1980s.

Early observers of the Guerin style of inter-personal relations noted the development of the relationship between the two. Some of her then colleagues noted – behind Veronica's almost exaggerated impulse to befriend – a kind of manipulation.

'She was,' said one such colleague who followed her path from the time she left school to the time she died, 'one of the most manipulative people I ever met. She would target people's weakest spots and most people's weakest spot is their insecurity. She would flatter them, tell them they were fantastic . . . so they were attracted to her and grateful to her. She did that with lots of people – including Haughey. Most of them fell for it.'

But many others saw the 'manipulation' as simply Veronica's innate friendliness and generosity. This latter quality was also much remarked upon; many of her friends and colleagues have recalled numerous little acts of kindness from her. Overall, what struck people were her remarkable 'people skills'.

Newspaper reports about Veronica Guerin's activities after she left school in the mid-1970s are confused. *The Irish Times* reported that she 'studied accountancy at Trinity College, Dublin, before joining her father's accountancy firm, Guerin and Reid, in Gardiner Street'.[1]

There are several other reports of her accountancy training, but none of them state definitively what, if any, exams she passed. The *Sunday Independent* wrote that she had trained to become an accountant, studying at college while she worked with her father in his Gardiner Street practice.[2]

Trinity College looked through their records and found no record of her having studied there.

Jimmy Guerin says that Veronica never studied accountancy. He thinks she might have taken one exam, but he is adamant that she had no professional qualification whatsoever.

She left full-time education after the Leaving Certificate, taken at 17 or 18, and went to work for the Irish League of Credit Unions. About one year later, she became an employee in her father's practice in a clerical position. There she picked up basic book-keeping and other accountancy skills, but that appears to have been the summit of her training.

A former colleague from her time in Fianna Fáil points to Veronica Guerin herself as the source of much of this 'confusion'. At some point in the early 1980s, when Veronica was working for Fianna Fáil, she told a blatant lie about her qualifications. 'She came in one day and told us that she'd

1 June 17 1996.
2 October 6 1996.

17

just passed her accountancy exams. She said she'd come top of the class and that she was the youngest person in Ireland to get them. We bought her presents to celebrate. Later we found out that it was all a lie; she'd never sat the exams at all.'

For her Fianna Fáil colleagues, it was the first indication that Veronica Guerin's relationship with the truth could be tenuous. It was also an early indication of Veronica's attachment to the notion of expediency – that the end always justified the means.

Christopher Guerin died suddenly in 1981. His death devastated the family. According to the *Sunday Independent*, 'Veronica found herself unable to continue in the same career. She found the thought of going back to accountancy distressing; she would have had to operate from her father's office, talk to her father's clients, live a life of constant, everyday reminders. She decided to quit . . . Veronica decided to study to become a public relations consultant.'[3]

The truth was somewhat different. After Christopher Guerin died, Jimmy Guerin was appointed as one of the executors of his estate. He decided to dispose of his late father's practice, since none of his siblings were trained accountants. The practice was sold about two months later. Veronica and her brother Martin Guerin, who had also worked for his father, lost their jobs.

But by this stage Veronica Guerin had become intimately involved with Fianna Fáil and had worked hard for the Dublin North Central candidates in the first of the two general elections in 1982. Her closeness and loyalty to Haughey was rewarded – in 1982 – with an appointment to the Governing Body of the National Institute of Higher Education in Glasnevin, Dublin.[4]

Most of the country's state and semi-state boards are stuffed with political supporters of whatever party is in power, but Veronica Guerin's appointment was, even by the

3 October 6 1996.
4 Now the Dublin City University.

normal standards of patronage, unusual.

At 24, she was the youngest board member. She had no professional or academic qualifications – apart from her Leaving Certificate – yet the brief biographical note that accompanied the announcement of her appointment stated that she was an 'Accountant, practising with Guerin and Reid & Co'. The letters CPA – Certified Public Accountant – were attached to her name.

But Veronica Guerin was not a Certified Public Accountant. At my request, the Institute of Certified Public Accountants checked their records and confirmed this. According to the Institute, it takes a minimum of five years' study and work experience to qualify as a CPA. A student who begins to study for the professional qualification straight from completing secondary education takes on average seven years to complete the course requirements.

Graduates in a relevant discipline are exempted from taking some of the Institute exams, but they still have to spend on average another two to three years in study before they are fully qualified.

All the other 24 members of the 1982–1987 Governing Body (apart from two student representatives) had strong academic credentials and/or relevant professional experience. They included Dr Edward Walsh, BE, MS, PhD, MIEE, MIEEE, the President of the NIHE's sister college in Limerick; John J. Kelly, BE, PhD., CEng, MIEI, FI Chem E, F Inst Pet, the Dean of the Faculty of Engineering and Architecture at University College, Dublin; Michael O'Donnell, M Econ Sc, BE, BComm, CEng, MI Prod E, MIEI, the Principal of the College of Technology, Bolton Street, Dublin and Peter Gallagher, BA, CCCE, MA (Ed), the Principal of Letterkenny Regional Technical College in Donegal.

The only member with no tertiary academic qualifications was Carol Moffett, Managing Director of Moffett Engineering, one of the most successful Irish businesses in recent years.

But Veronica was apparently undaunted by the qualifications of her colleagues on the NIHE. Dr Danny O'Hare, Head of the then NIHE and currently Head of Dublin City

University, recalls that she applied herself to her board work with great diligence.

> She was one of the very best attenders. Apart from the student representatives, she was by far the youngest member but that didn't stop her from querying things, expressing opinions, getting involved. I knew very little about her background. There was talk about accountancy and public relations; she said she was doing a Masters degree at the Dublin Institute of Technology.
>
> It was very clear that she was very friendly with Charlie Haughey. She also talked about meeting Gerry Adams, President of Sinn Fein, and Ray MacSharry.[5] She would often offer to liaise with Ministers, but I formed the opinion that she was more of a happy helper in the party than anything else.

Given her lack of experience, Veronica's impact on the board was exceptional. O'Hare says that he felt very positively towards Veronica. 'She was a sharp person . . . quite shrewd. She was very good on inter-personal issues.'

O'Hare believes that what drove her was 'being close to power, to where it's exercised, where deals are made. But I never got a sense of mission as such.'

In 1983 – one year after her appointment to NIHE – Veronica Guerin went on the Fianna Fáil payroll. She was appointed as an assistant to the Fianna Fáil delegation to the New Ireland Forum negotiations – the attempt by nationalist parties in the North and South to agree a common agenda.

Veronica threw herself into her work with characteristic enthusiasm. Her specific role was to liaise between the political parties. She worked out of the Fianna Fáil rooms on the fifth floor of Leinster House and at Dublin Castle, where the negotiations took place.

But by now some of her colleagues in Fianna Fáil were becoming increasingly wary of Veronica. There were doubts

5 A former Fianna Fáil minister and European commissioner.

about her qualifications. It was known that she had obtained accountancy work on the basis of her supposed qualifications, and had got into difficulties with one client.

Veronica was also developing an interest in journalism. She had met and become friendly with journalist Paddy Prendiville in circumstances outlined in the next chapter. Prendiville was then working for the *Sunday Tribune* newspaper under the editorship of Vincent Browne.

Prendiville shared Veronica Guerin's passion for politics, and throughout the course of the Forum negotiations, there was a steady drip-feed of stories from Guerin to Prendiville.

Much of it was trivial – Veronica did not have access to everything – but on one occasion, she did hand over a sensitive document which was published in full the following week in the *Sunday Tribune*. The article, which appeared on February 12 1984, was described in the *Sunday Tribune* as a 'draft report' on the New Ireland Forum and proposed, according to the *Tribune*, that a British and Irish joint authority commission, appointed by the London and Dublin governments, should run Northern Ireland. Paddy Prendiville, noted that this proposal was being 'vigorously opposed by Fianna Fáil'.

At least one person in Fianna Fáil suspected that Veronica was the source of this and other leaks. The suspicion surrounding her increased some time later when early morning cleaners in Leinster House came upon Veronica in Charles Haughey's private office; she appeared to be going through some of his files.

The cleaners reported the incident to Haughey's then private secretary, Catherine Butler. Butler confronted Veronica, who said that she was simply looking for something in a hurry. But Butler ordered that all the offices should be locked from then on.

The New Ireland Forum came to an end in May 1984, with the publication of its report. Veronica's contract with the party was terminated and never renewed. For a short period afterwards, she continued to come into the Leinster House offices at will, until an instruction was given to Leinster

House staff by a party official to deny her access unless she signed in as a visitor and was escorted through the building.

Veronica ceased to work for the Fianna Fáil party at that point, but she did continue to do some work for Charles Haughey's son Seán, who was trying to win a Dáil seat – which he later did. But her former Leinster House colleagues found out that Veronica was still claiming to be employed by them. Calls would come in for her to their offices long after she had left.

Veronica then decided to go into business on her own. In May 1984, she formed a public relations company, Guerin Public Relations Limited.

According to records held in the Companies Office, two people were named as directors – Veronica Guerin, described as an accountant, and Raymond Brannigan, described as a company director. David Thorby, with an address at Shanliss Avenue in Whitehall, was named as company secretary.

Brannigan was Veronica Guerin's brother-in-law. I have been unable to trace David Thorby or find anyone who knew him. He does not live, and never has lived, at the address given at Shanliss Avenue. The people who now live there bought the house three or four years ago. According to neighbours, who have lived on Shanliss Avenue for twenty years, an elderly lady lived in the house before the young couple moved in. They had never heard of David Thorby. There is no telephone listing for anyone named Thorby in Ireland – north or south.

According to the company files, Thorby and Brannigan resigned as director and company secretary respectively in 1985. They were replaced by Veronica Guerin and Graham Turley. Turley was described as a carpenter and company director.

According to Jimmy Guerin, the company was not a success. Veronica did acquire a few clients, but much of her work involved catering for various functions around the city. The work gradually petered out. The company was listed as 'dissolved' in 1992. No company accounts appear to have been filed.

Veronica and Graham Turley were married in 1985. The

reception was held in the Gresham Hotel in Dublin. It was a very lavish affair, according to some of the guests. Charlie Haughey attended, as did several members of his family.

In 1987, Guerin began a one-year graduate diploma course in marketing management at the Dublin Institute of Technology. The title of the course suggests that students have to be graduates, but according to DIT, two or three places are reserved every year for non-graduates with either an entrepreneurial or other relevant background.

Student files are destroyed after three years. It was not possible to discover how Veronica Guerin had obtained entry to the course. But once on it, as in other areas of her life, she excelled. Out of a class of 23 students, three of whom had Masters degrees, Veronica came in the first five in the final exams.

One lecturer describes her as 'intellectually able', and also popular: 'She was very good and generous with other students, especially with accountancy subjects. I think she qualified as an accountant. She had the most positive energy of anyone I've ever met. She was a wonderful person, with fantastic people skills.'

After the course Veronica returned to her PR work for a number of years. By this stage she was beginning to develop a real interest in journalism and was cultivating friends in the media.

At around this time an incident also took place that would later change the course of her career in journalism. It was something that would, a few years later, effectively force her to leave the first newspaper she ever worked for, the *Sunday Business Post*.

At some point in the late 1980s Veronica had begun to do some consultancy work for a small British airline which went out of business in 1990. The airline was looking for passenger handling rights at Dublin airport and was negotiating for this concession with Aer Rianta, the Irish aviation authority, and with the relevant government department.

Veronica became, in effect, the airline's Dublin representative. Negotiations were ongoing. At one stage, the airline's head office told the government department that Aer Rianta had agreed to give them the passenger handling rights.

The department asked Aer Rianta if this was the case. Aer Rianta denied it, contacted the airline and asked for an explanation. The company told Aer Rianta that they had been assured by their Dublin representative, whom they named as Veronica Guerin, that the rights had been granted.

In evidence, they produced a copy of a letter, purportedly signed by the Chief Executive of Aer Rianta, Derek Keogh, and printed on Aer Rianta-headed notepaper. The letter was to Veronica Guerin, and the contents were to the effect that Aer Rianta was about to grant the company's request.

The signature was a forgery. The writing, according to Aer Rianta sources, 'matched that of Veronica's'. Aer Rianta told the company that it was a fake, but decided to take no action against Veronica. They do not know what action, if any, the now-defunct airline took against her.

The incident would be resurrected some years later, when Veronica had left public relations for a career in journalism, with very dramatic results.

Some in Aer Rianta were not surprised at what had happened. Prior to the airline incident, Veronica had approached Aer Rianta with a view to acting as a consultant, to sort out a dispute between the company and a group of people with homes close to Dublin airport. The residents wanted money from Aer Rianta to compensate them for the nuisance likely to be caused by a proposed new runway.

Two Aer Rianta officials met with Veronica for preliminary discussions.

Afterwards, one of the officials went to check on something that had been bothering him throughout the meeting. Veronica's married name, he had discovered, was Turley. It was under that name that she had also made a claim for compensation as a member of the residents' group. Aer Rianta declined to avail of her services.

Veronica also worked for a time with a well-known and long-established Dublin travel agency, Club Travel, owned by businessman Liam Lonergan. It is not clear what the nature of her work was or how the association ended. When contacted for this book, Mr Lonergan would only say that she worked with the company, adding, curiously: 'I don't want to enter any discussion on the subject.'

Veronica was now about to join the world of journalism. The dare-devil, risk-taking child was clearly becoming a dare-devil adult, in a world where the risks were higher. She was ambitious, restless, determined and with a ruthless streak.

She was a woman who was also charming, talented but capable of duplicity, a woman who did not always put limits on how far she was prepared to go, a woman whose professional dealings had been highly questionable. Her interaction with the world of journalism was likely to be, at least, interesting; at most, dangerous.

3

FATAL ATTRACTION – THE ORIGINS

Jimmy Guerin does not remember Veronica as having had early journalistic ambitions.

'She never thought about what she wanted to be when she grew up; we never really discussed it, even when she was doing her leaving [exams]; she didn't give a shit.'

Jimmy Guerin found no obvious pattern to the career moves his sister took. 'Completely inconsistent. Jumping from Jack to Billy and Billy to Jack, until she found something, and that was in journalism.'

He speaks plainly about the reasons why journalism attracted his sister.

'An awful lot of journalism has a certain amount of bull-shit, and she was able to mix it with people.' Journalism's erratic demands suited her too. 'She found it much easier to work the undisciplined hours, as opposed to going to a job from nine to five – which she couldn't hack.'

According to Jimmy, the first story she wrote was on Aer Lingus holidays, a story he believes she happened upon through contacts she had established when she was in Fianna Fáil. He describes her early stories as 'fairly explosive'.

Veronica certainly took pleasure in her success, even, according to Jimmy, having her first few front-page stories block-mounted and put on the wall.

She began with business stories. She'd had an unfortunate time in business herself, absolutely disastrous. Then she did the story on Aer Lingus holidays . . . about fraud . . . and she knew how to track and how to chase it. When she was working with my father in accountancy, she [had to] check the invoice against the payment, against the bank statement, so she had the basic training in how to follow things. This was why she was able to delve into matters in various stories so easily . . . she knew where to go and where to look.

Jimmy believes that Veronica's interest in crime grew out of this initial interest in the business world. In the early nineties, the Irish government instituted a tax amnesty which benefited many known criminals. This event, according to Jimmy, sparked Veronica's first interest in the underworld.

Paddy Prendiville had known Veronica Guerin for about fourteen years before she died. When they first met in the early 1980s, he was working for the *Sunday Tribune*. Later he became editor of *Phoenix* magazine, the Irish equivalent of *Private Eye*. The magazine had long been a trenchant critic of the *Sunday Independent*'s politics in particular and its journalism in general. None the less, he had actually encouraged her to join the paper in 1994. He was also instrumental in bringing about her entry into journalism in 1990. This is what he remembers.

A group of Young Liberals had come over from England in 1983. One of them that I'd known for an age rang me up and said would I go and meet him for a drink. He had a meeting with Fianna Fáil people, with Ógra Fianna Fáil.

So I went down and in the middle of this session, one of the Young Liberals said, 'There's no difference between Fine Gael and Fianna Fáil.' So I jumped in on my third pint and said, 'Hold on a second,' and then I gave my republican analysis – of Fianna Fáil being the party for the workers and the small farmers, whereas Fine Gael, at bottom, was the party for the professionals.

And suddenly I could feel these eyes staring at me. It was Veronica – I had never met her before. And she said, 'Are you a journalist? The *Sunday Tribune* isn't it?'

27

She rang me afterwards, and made it very clear first of all that we were frogspawn as far as she was concerned. She was fascinated by me, but she said she hated all journalists, because of what they were doing to Charlie Haughey . . . As far as she was concerned, we were all Dublin 4 types, Fine Gael blue shirts, and so on.[1]

But she was mesmerised by me because I didn't fit into that, at least not intellectually. And she cultivated me and we cultivated each other for our own immediate, selfish, opportunist goals. She would tell me stories from Fianna Fáil, for example.

But she was fascinated, I'm very clear about saying it, she was fascinated by the media from the very first moment I met her. She was fascinated, and she wanted to be a journalist, but she would not admit it.

Prendiville encouraged her to write, but her first piece of work for him – an article on the Fianna Fáil TD Ivor Callely – met with some degree of scorn.

'It was the funniest thing I've ever read . . . stuff like "Ivor is not only talented, he's hardworking too." We couldn't use it.'

Through Fianna Fáil and through her chance meeting with Paddy Prendiville, Veronica was making her first tentative steps into the world of journalism. The political contacts she had made were already being used. Her passion for, and her almost romantic view, of the profession was also becoming evident. Until her death, she lost neither.

1 Dublin's liberal intelligentsia, so named because of the postal district in which many of them live.

4

MADNESS AND METHOD

'She didn't see any great need to examine the methodology
she used to procure information.'

Damien Kiberd

Damien Kiberd is the editor, co-founder and formerly part-
owner of the *Sunday Business Post*. The weekly newspaper
was first published in 1989 and has been one of the few new
media successes in Ireland in recent years. It specialises in
business news, but also has a strong political core. It is one of
just a handful of Irish newspapers that has no links with
Independent Newspapers. In August 1997 the paper was sold
to Trinity Holdings for £5.5 million.

Editorially, it is the polar opposite of the *Sunday
Independent*. It strongly supports the nationalist view of
Northern Ireland, and is very supportive of the peace process.
It has resisted the tabloidisation of much of the rest of the
Irish Sunday newspaper market and appears almost ascetic
in comparison. Its politics would have found an echo in
Veronica's, as would its editorial focus on business news. It
was to this paper that Veronica came in 1990, looking for her
first journalistic assignment.

Kiberd recalls that Veronica had sent a CV into the newspaper and paid a visit in 1990, shortly after the birth of her
son Cathal. She had been up-front about her reasons for
approaching the *Business Post* – it was a new newspaper, and
she felt it might be amenable to giving her a start.

Veronica struck Kiberd as very genuine, though he admits

29

that she 'needed to be shown about journalism, how to write for newspapers.'

Kiberd did not give Veronica a job straight away. He agreed to her writing an article about aeroplane leasing – a hot topic in the business world at the time – and she had impressed him with her understanding of the subject. 'She wrote a very good piece about aircraft leasing, though the literary style of it was very unsuited to newspapers.'

After that, Veronica continued to file stories on a sporadic and freelance basis – sometimes doing more, sometimes less. This work was her introduction to the world of investigative journalism.

Kiberd recalls her interest in the Aer Lingus holidays scandal – the source of her first 'big' stories. Aer Lingus had a subsidiary, Aer Lingus Holidays, which ran charter tours to the Mediterranean and other destinations. It was the market leader, and each year as the company applied for the renewal of its operator licence to the Department of Aviation, it showed a profit.

In reality, Aer Lingus Holidays was losing a fortune and the losses were being covered up. The reason the market leader was losing money was because, in order to dominate the marketplace, it was undercutting all its competitors.

Veronica's findings were subsequently borne out in a report by Price Waterhouse consultants. She also made a documentary on the affair with RTE, but this ended in dispute.[1] Veronica made the information over to Kiberd and it was published, marking her triumphant debut in business journalism.

Another early success for Veronica was her investigation into Irish businessman Larry Goodman, whose group of companies had gone into receivership.[2] Goodman's business

---

1 According to RTE, the row was over Veronica's role in the televised report. They wanted someone else to present the story; she insisted that it should be herself. In the end, she abandoned the project and took the story to the *Sunday Business Post*.
2 Goodman was the country's largest beef producer.

interests became seriously afflicted through the disruption of the Middle Eastern market by the Gulf War, and he had become heavily indebted to the banks.

Veronica found that Goodman had given £25 million of company money to two men in Cyprus. The money had effectively become frozen in a bank in the west of Cyprus.

Veronica, still a freelance journalist, went to Cyprus to investigate. 'That was the way she worked; she wouldn't even tell you what she was doing. She was saying she was working on a story and the next day you'd get a phone call from Nicosia.'

Kiberd found this degree of dedication impressive, but extraordinary. The rewards for such stories were not vast. 'Five hundred pounds – or a thousand if she'd put a lot of effort into it. But it certainly wouldn't have been enough to pay for air fares to go to wherever.'

Kiberd also reports Veronica tracking down a man in Tipperary, a farmer called Joe Kenny, who had been involved in the Cyprus money transaction, and many other unusual business deals.

It was her energy and drive that seemed so remarkable to her first editor. The fact of her having powerful contacts was not so surprising. Kiberd knew that she had many contacts in Fianna Fáil, including Charles Haughey. 'What struck me, was that she definitely wanted to be at the centre of the action; she had a nose for a story from the beginning. She had no real interest in doing the sort of mundane or pedestrian work that other rookie journalists do for years.'

Right from the start, Veronica evinced a high level of ambition, combined with an ability to keep matters close to her chest. 'She exuded a sense of mystery about various stories. She wouldn't normally tell you about how she got her information; you'd discover afterwards how she procured information on some occasions and she liked to be a figure of mystery. She deliberately cultivated that kind of image.'

Damien Kiberd agreed to tell me the story about Veronica's dealings with Aer Rianta, alluded to earlier in this book. He had decided, he said, the night before my interview took place, to put it on the record. He told me that if I was going to tell the truth in my book, then it was essential that I knew the ins and outs of the Aer Rianta story.

She came up with a remarkable story about Aer Rianta's attempts to secure new duty-free outlets abroad. She had actually got minutes of meetings of the board of directors of Aer Rianta or Aer Rianta International, at which they'd discussed the potential embarrassment of this.

I asked her, prior to running the story, to get some sort of comment from Aer Rianta on their version of the story. We did run one story, to the effect that Aer Rianta was involved in making payments offshore to procure contracts in Third-World countries. Then she had come up with the detailed information about the discussion at board level, which was absolute rocket fuel from the journalistic point of view.

Kiberd suggested that Veronica put the matter to Aer Rianta. They responded by seeking, both corporately and on behalf of a number of their individual directors, an injunction against the *Sunday Business Post*. As is normal in such cases, the courts granted an interim injunction to the plaintiffs.

The injunction was granted on a Saturday, and as a result the *Sunday Business Post* was forced to publish with blank spaces across its front page, stating only the word 'Injuncted'.

A solution was eventually agreed. The *Sunday Business Post* would desist from publishing the information that it had in its possession about Aer Rianta's overseas dealings, and Aer Rianta would desist from all actions against the *Sunday Business Post*, including the threatened libel actions which they had begun.

But while both sides were in the courthouse, awaiting the hearing, the counsel for Aer Rianta produced an affidavit, which they said they intended to read in court. This affidavit could have had a highly damaging effect on Veronica, both personally and as a journalist.

Aer Rianta claimed, in this affidavit, that Veronica was

pursuing a vendetta against Aer Rianta, and that this vendetta arose from issues which predated her entry into the world of journalism.

They said that when she had been working as a public relations consultant, in order to impress her clients – who were a small airline, overseas-owned – that she had actually forged letters from Aer Rianta to herself, on Aer Rianta-headed notepaper, which gave the impression that she somehow had an 'in' with senior people in Aer Rianta, and was in a position to deliver concessions relating to the management of planes at Dublin airport.

Veronica denied that the claims made in the affidavit were true. But Kiberd pointed out that the consequences of going into court, and of the reading of the affidavit, could throw very grave doubt on her motivation in pursuing the Aer Rianta overseas story. 'I had no doubt that her Aer Rianta story was true, but given that they had assembled a top class legal team, involving at least two or three senior counsel . . . they would throw whatever muck they had at her, and play fast and loose with her reputation.'

Veronica announced herself prepared to face them down. But Kiberd thought this unwise – not just for his newspaper, but for his journalist. 'The credibility of the newspaper would be at stake, but more particularly, her personal credibility would be at stake.'

But Veronica, showing that same single-mindedness of which her every acquaintance speaks, insisted on going into court, and denying the truth of the allegations in the affidavit. 'I felt absolutely devastated on that day when we were sitting in the basement of the High Court. But Veronica, being Veronica, wanted to go ahead with it.'

In the end, however, Kiberd told me, the decision had gone beyond Veronica's remit. Agreements not to publish and not to proceed were immediately entered into. Kiberd and his colleagues were devastated.

I did discuss the matter with Veronica but after what had happened, the relationship between Veronica and the paper was coloured by this whole experience.

[We had been] putting ourselves forward as proponents of freedom of the press and the right of access to public information, yet the ground had been pulled from underneath us, as a result of information which we were completely unaware of until the day we walked into the court.

Veronica still stuck to her story, and denied the accusations made by Aer Rianta. But Kiberd had seen the letters, and knew that they were clearly forgeries.

'Derek Keogh was the chief executive and it was his signature that had been forged. Now I've no proof that Veronica forged it, but it certainly wasn't Derek Keogh's signature.'

She stayed with the *Sunday Business Post*, but with her reputation compromised in the eyes of those who employed her. Kiberd admits to being worried by Veronica's ruthlessness in pursuit of information. 'I think it's fair to say that she didn't see any great need to examine the methodology she used to procure information.'

'For example, let's say that you as Emily O'Reilly, political correspondent, were investigating a political story; you would ring up the politician and see if the politician would speak to you. But would you go to the schoolyard of the politician's ten-year-old daughter and ask the politician's daughter if there was another politician in her father's house last night, and what were they talking about?'[3]

As Kiberd sees it, Veronica lacked a sense of judgement or proportion in relation to the methodology of her information-gathering. Integrity in the pursuit of a story is, ultimately, as

3 In the course of researching a political story, Veronica had approached the daughter of a politican and told her, untruthfully, that she, Veronica, had been present at a meeting at the child's father's house some time before. She prompted the child to remember who else had been at this meeting. The child insisted that she did not remember Veronica having been at the house.

important as the truths being sought. Dubious reporting tactics reflect badly on the newspapers.

But Kiberd is full of praise for Veronica's work, and notes that a number of her stories were 'absolutely superb'. He also notes that she began to develop an interest in crime reporting while working for the *Sunday Business Post*. She had conducted an investigation into the murder of an underworld figure called Travers, whose death was followed by a spate of killings.

Kiberd had a little information on the subject from some of his own contacts, and passed it on to Veronica. 'Her eyes lit up . . . she seemed to think this would be a great story. She spent about three or four days going around talking to fellas who had been in contact with Travers and she came up with quite a good, full-page story about the death of this man and why it had occurred.'

As well as being her first major crime story, this was the last major piece Veronica wrote for the *Sunday Business Post*. Kiberd suggests that, in addition to the question mark over her reputation after the Aer Rianta affair, Veronica may have felt that she had put the newspaper under a lot of pressure, by attracting legal writs in relation to stories she had written.

At the time, Kiberd believes, the *Sunday Tribune* was approaching Veronica to write for it. Given that her freelance earnings from the *Business Post* were scarcely adequate recompense for the effort she invariably put in on her stories, he was not surprised when she left.

But her parting was amicable, and she was missed. 'Even in spite of the Aer Rianta thing, we were very sad to see her leave and join the *Tribune*, because she was a great asset to our newspaper. And she was a very pleasant and lively person, and great fun. You never knew what she was going to come up with.'

Veronica left the *Sunday Business Post* in the spring of 1993. Few people inside the newspaper and exceptionally few outside knew about the Aer Rianta incident, or were aware of the manner in which she occasionally practised her journalism. She was a journalist who got great stories; nobody thought to look any further.

Just as no one in the *Sunday Business Post* was aware of the misrepresentation of her professional qualifications in her earlier life, of the breaking of trust with some in Fianna Fáil through the incident with Charlie Haughey's private files, no one at her next career stop knew or would know about the truth behind the Aer Rianta injunction.

The Aer Rianta incident seriously compromised Veronica's professional integrity. The approach to the politician's child was also dubious; involving children in stories – using them in this instance to research a story likely to damage the child's father – is an unacceptable, exploitative practice. But Veronica was living up to the standard she had set herself: that she would go anywhere, do anything, for a story.

So, by the time Veronica left the *Sunday Business Post*, there was a body of evidence to show that she had the kind of characteristics that, if unchecked, can lead people into serious trouble. Combined with the 'Walter Mitty' element in her psychological make-up, there was an apparent blindness to the ethics and consequences of some of her actions.

But very few people were aware of those flaws. Few, if any, of the people she befriended during her years in journalism knew the full story. None of the stories travelled. When she later quit the *Sunday Tribune* and moved to the *Sunday Independent*, her new bosses thought they were simply acquiring a brilliant journalist, with an enviable record of scoops. All that was true, but behind that success was a complex and worrying array of motive and method.

In the *Sunday Independent*, Veronica Guerin would not just report crime; she would enter the world of the criminal. She would befriend some, invite at least one to her home, play one off against the other and go on assignments to meet them in the company of her young son.

She would allow herself to be used for their own, deadly agendas and for the benefit of the Gardaí and her newspaper. In the end, the criminals killed her because she had entered too far into their world and she was now an irritant that they had to eradicate.

In the end, she would die because nobody took it upon themselves to force her to stop. The *Sunday Independent*, week after week, would publish the results of her deep, dangerous, thrilling and ultimately deadly flirtation with dysfunctional, criminal, men.

As she edged closer and closer to her death, her profile would become even higher; her voice and face marketed constantly on radio and television, as she repeated again and again her determination not be intimidated, not to stop.

Some months after she was killed, a speaker at a seminar in memory of Veronica in Dublin remarked that whenever a journalist is murdered, the journalist is eventually blamed for his or her own death. Yet to date, Veronica Guerin's death has been treated as an abstract event. Veronica herself has been depicted as a cartoon cut-out – a veritable Lois Lane: the one-dimensional, fearless reporter who met her end at the hands of ruthless men. Hollywood has loved that; indeed they are making the movie already.

Few people have asked why it was Veronica who died. Few people asked why it was that *this* journalist got so close, that *this* journalist made the criminals angry enough or scared enough to kill her?

Part of the answer, the part that no one speaks of, lies in Veronica's psychology and the clues to that are everywhere, from the lies she told about her accountancy qualifications, to her dubious practice of public relations to her early adventures in journalism, to the bizarre manner in which she conducted herself after the initial attacks on her.

Everyone who knew Veronica liked her; it was impossible not to be drawn to a woman who was charming, lively, good company, and generous. But many people who knew her professionally did not trust her, and were appalled by the lengths to which she would go to achieve her ends.

In themselves, many of the breaches of integrity she committed were trivial. But cumulatively, they point to an individual who not only took unacceptable risks, but whose professional operations were unstable and unethical.

Veronica had passed through two newspapers before she began working for the *Sunday Independent*. She had left under a cloud on both occasions, but few were privy to the real reasons for her departures. Perhaps she should have been sacked from those newspapers because of how she had behaved. But she wasn't, because she was liked. Popular on a personal level, she also wrote good stories, and in the hugely competitive world of newspaper publishing, that mattered. Blind eyes were turned.

5

AN AURA OF MYSTERY

Veronica went to work for the *Sunday Tribune* in the spring of 1993. Her output and her energy were remarkable. The hallmarks of her working style were all present from the first day: she rarely went into the office; she worked alone and many of her stories were secured by door-stepping the individuals involved.

It was during her time at the *Tribune* that she may have met the criminal who would later become one of her primary sources on the *Sunday Independent* – John Traynor. This period marked another step along the road to her total immersion in the world of Dublin crime.

Alan Byrne was Veronica's news editor when she worked on the *Sunday Tribune*. He now edits the *Racing Post* in London. He became very close to Veronica and was one of those who expressed serious concern about her safety in the weeks before she died.

He guards her memory carefully. Before we began the interview, he said that he would say nothing that would hurt her husband, Graham Turley.

Byrne recalls her coming in one Saturday, and being told by a colleague that she wouldn't come up to see him in his office because she was scared of the editor, Vincent Browne. Years later, Veronica denied the implication hotly. It is difficult to imagine her being scared.

After that first meeting, Byrne reports, the *Tribune* came to rely progressively on Veronica for many of its stories. He too reports a unique impulsiveness, tenacity and mystery about her reporting style.

> Her way of operating was either to get tip-offs herself or find leads. She'd ask if she should start looking into something, and then she'd disappear for a few days. She'd ring in occasionally, reasonably regularly and then she'd appear on Saturday afternoon or Saturday evening with the story, and we'd have to spend quite a bit of time having it checked for libel and so on.

Byrne suggests that she was unique among journalists: 'she would go and stake out places, or sit and wait for people to come home if they weren't there. Other journalists would ring someone up and if there was no reply, they'd just say "I couldn't get them." But Veronica would go out to the house, sit there for hours and hours and hours, wait for the person to come home and then go and attempt to interview them.'

While most stories in most newspapers are often comparatively 'instant' – a matter of hours between conference and filed copy – Veronica tended to pursue several stories with varying degrees of intensity, building them up to completion over a number of weeks.

'She did tend to work alone; she also obviously had many very well-placed contacts, who would tip her off about things or from whom she would extract information and she would then go off and beaver away on that particular story.'

Byrne admits that, at that time, good stories seemed thin on the ground. Once she was hired, he came to rely more and more on Veronica to carry the day with a good story.

'A lot of what she did, she did on her own initiative. I think the Eamonn Casey story was one of the few stories where she was encouraged to do it by us. It was clearly the biggest story in Irish journalism at the time.'[1]

Her methods, he says, were certainly unusual by comparison with other journalists. 'It's unusual to face down people

---

1 Bishop Eamonn Casey, who fathered a child and fled to South America when this was disclosed.

to the extent that she did, in terms of confronting them at their homes. She would refuse to take no for an answer.

She was often secretive about the sources of her stories, and occasionally she had prior knowledge of things that were about to happen. 'She'd know if they were going to arrest somebody or take a particular initiative. It's hard to know whether she had one exceptional Gardaí contact or half a dozen.'

Byrne too pays tribute to Veronica's networking skills, and cites these as integral to her success. 'She would remember names; she would talk to people, even going to football matches. Just walking to a football match, she'd know so many people on the way.'

Byrne last saw Veronica around three weeks before she died, at the beginning of June 1996, having gone to a friendly match between Croatia and Ireland at Lansdowne Road. Beforehand, he met Veronica for a drink in a nearby hotel. 'And even sitting there for just twenty minutes, the number of people who walked by that she knew was amazing. She was a phenomenal networker and she had a remarkable skill to gain people's confidence and get people to talk to her.'

He reports a similar level of connectedness when he and others went with Veronica to the United States for the 1994 World Cup.

'Even in the *Tribune* I used to tease her that on Saturday evenings, after that very frantic period when the paper is going to press and everybody is either sitting around or gone to the pub, I used to tease her that she'd be working the room like a Fianna Fáil councillor.'

It never seemed to Byrne that there was any agenda behind Veronica's friendliness. 'If somebody mentioned that their mother was ill, three weeks later she'd ask how she was. She just had that aptitude. I mean there wasn't too much to be gained in working a room full of reporters – they're not going to give her any stories. It was just a natural thing that she did.'

Her enthusiasm for her work, he feels, was possibly because she had come so late to journalism. 'She never really talked much about her accountancy career. She talked a bit, a little bit, about her term working with Fianna Fáil at the New Ireland Forum. I used to tease her about Charlie Haughey, but she wouldn't hear any criticism of him.'

Initially, Veronica was not overtly involved in crime work at the *Tribune*. She started out investigating financial scandals – some of which had a criminal element – but was not a crime reporter *per se*.

The biggest story she did for us was the Eamonn Casey interview, the second was Tara Mines,[2] and the third biggest was the James Livingstone interview, which obviously was a crime story.[3]

Then she wrote a story about the stolen Beit paintings[4]. *That* was a crime story and she had a fantastic inside track on it. She came up with information, in a relatively short space of time, which the rest of us wouldn't even have discovered after weeks of trying.

I suppose she gravitated towards crime because, by definition, it's where the bigger stories happen and if you want to do big stories, then it's an area that will yield results.

She liked teasing things out, with a thoroughness which few reporters would bother with. It might involve tracing irregular payments through various people or accounts.

Byrne reports that while most reporters spend 90 per cent of their time on the phone, Veronica actually went, in person, to the source of her stories. 'If there was somebody in Cork she wanted to interview, instead of ringing them and trying to get them on the phone, you'd get a call from her on the mobile saying, "I'm on my way to Cork." In some respects an inefficient method, but occasionally yielding high results.'

2 The story concerned contributions made by the company to politicians.
3 Dublin tax inspector James Livingstone had been questioned by the Gardaí in connection with the murder of his wife, Grace. Veronica also interviewed him. No one yet has been charged with her murder.
4 In September 1993, Veronica wrote the inside story of a covert police operation which had led to the recovery of the Beit family paintings – worth £35 million.

Byrne feels that, while not knowing any specific details, Veronica became progressively disenchanted with the *Tribune* at the same time as being head-hunted by the *Sunday Independent*. He also cites the deterioration of her relationship with Vincent Browne.

But I wouldn't have thought she was happy to go to the *Sunday Independent*. She was quite republican, quite nationalist and very Fianna Fáil in terms of her background. She would have had major reservations about much of the content of the paper.

But she felt there were two sides to the *Indo* and that she was operating in one sphere. She didn't agree with the other style of journalism practised in the paper, or endorse it, but she felt that her work could co-exist with it.

I think she loved the crime reporting there. She was doing what she wanted, and setting her own agenda to a large extent. Being given free rein and thriving on it.

Rory Godson was the business editor of the *Sunday Tribune* when Veronica joined the paper in 1993. They became good friends in and out of work.

She was immediately popular with her colleagues, says Godson, but parts of her life remained compartmentalised. She seemed enigmatic. 'We never quite knew where she worked from, whether it was her home, an office in Wicklow Street, an office on Fitzwilliam Square or her car.'

With insight, Godson suggests that the subterfuge may have been partly due to Veronica's insecurity over juggling the roles of journalist and mother. One's credibility, particularly in a male-dominated profession, can be better maintained if colleagues believe you might be out on a story, when actually you are home, tending to a sick toddler. Nevertheless, the net effect of Veronica's secrecy was, says Godson, to create an aura of mystery.

Like so many of her colleagues, Godson insists that there was something very different about Veronica, a quality that set her apart from other journalists. She would not merely come into the office, discuss her ideas, then go away and execute them as another reporter might. 'She would phone you, meet outside the office, discuss ten different stories, some of which were hard to follow. Then, late in the week, she would deliver a story, which sometimes had nothing to do with the first ten suggestions. This piece would arrive in typed on the reverse of her home headed paper or on floppy disc. Somewhere in it would be the best story in any Irish newspaper that week.'

Godson was intermittently Veronica's editor when he covered for Alan Byrne as news editor, or when she worked under him in his capacity as business editor. He reports that her working arrangement with the paper was imprecise. 'When she wrote in the business [section] I was never sure whether she was supposed to be paid extra. She would say: "Don't worry, I'm already working for a TV programme, so I'm being paid twice." '

Godson notes that she never filed expenses claims – there was a sense that Veronica was so fulfilled by her work, so driven by its demands and its rewards, that the money was incidental.

Godson also points out, though, that this unique sense of purpose had its darker side. 'She got stories because of raw determination and sometimes an indifference to the consequences for herself or for others of what she was doing. This also meant that there was a lack of perspective.'

When later they worked together on the *Sunday Independent*, Godson was impressed that none of this raw energy had dissipated as Veronica grew more experienced and accomplished.

'RTE's "Prime Time" had run a programme in which a chap called Pat Tuffy made bizarre claims against a person who, while not named, was identifiable as Michael Lowry, who was then a government minister.'

Veronica and Godson 'set to work on Tuffy'. She spent, he recalls, ten or twelve hours on November nights camped outside his house until eventually she saw him sneak round the side and followed him in. She interviewed him at length, taped it, transcribed it, and demonstrated all the holes in his story. Vast amounts of hours put into one single job – an input which earned her considerable respect.

On another occasion at the *Tribune*, she was working for me on a hugely complex story about the operation of a quarry in Cork. She called me from Dublin in the early evening about the story and I told her I would see her the next day.

Late that night, she called me and said she was just starting on the road from Cork back to Dublin and that she had been checking a detail on the story that was still weeks away from publication. In other words, at a moment's notice, she had left home on a seven-hour round-trip.

Godson's final memory of Veronica highlights just how single-minded, ruthless even, she could be in pursuit of her goals, both professional and personal. He was flying home from London on a Saturday night and met Veronica on the plane. At that time, both of them had been looking for tickets for the FA Cup Final for their mutual friend, Alan Byrne.

She sat beside me and she said: 'Do you know what? I got Alan his tickets, premium, best tickets in the house.' She said, 'Guess how I got them?' And all this was at the top of her voice; a lot of people were listening, because she was a famous person by now.

She said that there was this guy, whom we both knew vaguely, and he'd got on the plane that morning from Dublin to go to the Cup Final with his son, and just when they were about to take off, he got pains in his chest as though he was having a heart attack. He was taken off on a stretcher, clutching his chest. Veronica said she'd run after him and said, 'Johnny, this probably isn't the right time, but you and your son are getting off the plane and do you have any tickets for the match?'

He gave them to her and she took them. She was absolutely delighted with herself for having pulled this stroke.

The accounts of her early career, in politics, PR and in journalism, provide some telling insights into Veronica's character, and the manner in which it affected her practice of journalism. But it is impossible to tell the further story of Veronica Guerin without telling the story of the paper she worked and died for. In essence this story is the story of a fatal attraction. It is the story of what happened when a journalist who operated as Veronica did came to work for a newspaper that operated as the *Sunday Independent* did. It is impossible to see the story in any other light.

6

WATER-COOLER NEWS

Many things were whispered after Veronica Guerin's murder. At first people only whispered to spouses and very close friends, afraid that any deviation from the public story would lead to accusations of begrudgery, cynicism and jealousy.

The first person to raise his head above the parapet – *Irish Times* columnist Vincent Browne – was so comprehensively savaged that he was forced to apologise within days. Browne had been editor of the *Sunday Tribune* when Veronica had worked there.

Browne had suggested two things in his article. He wrote that Veronica's death might not have had anything to do with what she had written or was about to write. He also wrote that it was not the function of journalists to investigate crimes and criminals in the manner that Veronica had. He said that it was the job of journalists to hold institutions to account for their failure to tackle social problems, including crime.

Browne wrote: 'The killing of Veronica Guerin, outrageous, abominable and tragic though it may be in personal terms, in no way compromises the freedom of the press in holding institutions of power accountable.' He stressed that the investigation of crime was tangential to the main role of the press. The police, the courts and the prison system are in place to look after the abuse of power on the part of crime bosses. Journalism's business, meanwhile, is to hold these institutions accountable for the way they cope with the crime bosses and the crime phenomenon.

Browne's article appeared just two days after Veronica's

47

murder. Few people were receptive to his thesis that her activities were journalistically suspect. At that time, there was one story and one story only.

Some days later Browne apologised for his suggestion that her death may not have been directly linked to her work. He did not withdraw his comments about the proper role of journalism.

Browne's comments may have been badly timed and hence insensitive, but he was at least saying what he felt. Some people suspected his motivation. He and Veronica had parted on very bad terms during Browne's editorship of the *Sunday Tribune*, when Veronica had secured a major scoop by tracking down and later interviewing Bishop Eamonn Casey.

Casey was a high-profile member of the Irish hierarchy who had fled the country when *The Irish Times* had revealed that he had fathered a child sixteen years earlier. Veronica's scoop generated huge sales for the paper over a three-week period. It was the story that had brought her to public attention.

Both Guerin and Browne would later – privately – give radically different versions of what had happened during the lengthy period when the story was being researched.

Guerin left the newspaper shortly afterwards and was quickly signed up by the *Sunday Independent*, her first story appearing in January 1994. (Browne refused to give an interview for this book.)

When she died, the whispered media consensus – among those who did not work for the Independent Newspaper group – was that Veronica had chosen the wrong paper to die for. Had veteran war correspondent Robert Fisk been killed in Beirut while working for the *News of the World*, the reaction would have been similar.

No other publication in recent years has generated as much controversy in Ireland as the *Sunday Independent*. The newspaper was, and is, outstandingly successful, with a readership of over one million people in a country with a population of less than four million. Since late 1997, the paper has suffered a slight dip in sales, but it is still a phenomenal publishing success.

Prior to the appointment of long-time *Independent* staffer Aengus Fanning as editor in the mid-1980s, there was little that was remarkable about the *Sunday Independent*. Its politics were slightly right of centre; it was hostile to republican sentiments, but it rarely produced anything that disturbed the political, social or economic status quo.

Fanning threw out the rule book. He eschewed the paper's old conventions of balance and public service journalism and with the appointment of the former woman's magazine editor Anne Harris as features editor, turned a conventional newspaper into one of the biggest talking points in Irish public life.

The *Sunday Independent* is now a brash nineties mix of in-your-face reportage and icon-smashing commentary that makes compulsive reading. Like its ideological sister in the UK – the *Sunday Times* – it thrives on an intensely marketable mix of controversial editorial. It delights in taking the anti-consensual view on every subject from the ozone layer to Northern Ireland. To use former *Sunday Times* editor Andrew Neil's expression about his own editorial style of choice, it is 'contrarian'.

Its great gift is to perceive and serve up each Sunday a highly readable précis of what every office canteen has been buzzing with throughout the previous six days. In the United States they call it 'water-cooler news'. The editorial is highly personalised. It revels in taking an anti-PC approach.

The mix is also curiously un-Irish, in its public prurience, its delight in making the most savage and often unprovoked attacks on whomever has been chosen as that week's victim. At times when even its most loyal readers have felt that an article was over the top, Voltaire's famous attributed quote about not liking certain opinions but defending to the death a person's right to state them has been dusted down and made to guide every written word in the paper.

The more sacred the personage, the more savage the attack. In their time, prime ministers, ministers, cardinals, even the Nobel Prize-winning poet Seamus Heaney have been attacked by the *Sunday Independent*. Minor figures – innocent bystanders in the weekly *Sunday Independent* war against its market-generated enemies – are assailed if their politics are suspect, i.e nationalist.

In February 1994, the paper reached new standards of viciousness. Its target was a young woman called Courtney Kennedy, the daughter of Ethel Kennedy and the late Robert Kennedy.

Courtney had been an anonymous figure until she met and married a man called Paul Hill. Hill was one of the 'Guildford Four' – a group of Irishmen wrongly convicted of the 1970s' Guildford bombing in England. On his release, he still had to face an appeal against a 1974 murder charge. In the spring of 1994, that hearing began in Belfast.

Hill was accompanied to court by Courtney and other high-profile members of the Kennedy family. As Irish nationalist sympathisers, the Kennedy family were natural targets for the *Sunday Independent*. But they left to a woman contributor – who had specialised up until then in writing about her own, ultimately doomed romance with a Turkish man – the task of 'taking out' the family's weakest link – Courtney.

The article, by Molly McAnailly Burke, appeared with two other Kennedy family-linked articles on the same page – neither of them positive. She described Courtney as the 'plainest pudding to emerge from a world dynasty since "Thunder Thighs" Christina Onassis'.

'I would never have brought this up,' she went on to state, 'if it weren't that seeing Courtney's pasty mug all over the place standing by her man during his appeal against a 1974 murder conviction made me recall having met her in New York about six years ago. It was in Delia's nightclub, and upon hearing who she was, I was shockingly unimpressed. For Courtney, I'm sorry to say, was as ugly, graceless and gormless as she was snobbish, unfriendly and rude.'

The writer then mused about the likelihood of the marriage lasting, and whether they would start a family if and when Paul Hill's name was cleared.[1]

'Plain she may be,' the attack continued,

1 Paul and Courtney had a baby daughter in 1997.

but Courtney does come from considerable stock, most of whom were out in force in Belfast last week. Handsome Ethel Kennedy and blonde loudmouth Congressman Joe were flanked by stylish daughters and wives.

But it made buck-toothed Courtney's weaknesses stand out the more in the illustrious brood – an ugly duckling who has yet to sprout a single appealing feather in personality or wit. Money and pedigree can't buy you charm.

The editor of the *Sunday Independent* has occasionally said that he never tells his columnists what to write about. If six of them end up attacking the same person on the same day, then this is pure coincidence. Yet the phenomenon of everyone singing from the same hymn sheet is relentless. The journalists seem to know what is going to tickle the editor's fancy from week to week; after a while they do not have to be told.

It is never clear whether the agenda being pursued is that of the Independent group's wealthy, colourful and charismatic chairman, Tony O'Reilly or Dr A.J.F. O'Reilly as all the Independent titles deferentially call him – the doctorate received from the University of Bradford in 1980 for a thesis he submitted on the launch of Kerrygold butter.

The brashness and power of his newspaper group is a reflection of the man himself. For several decades, O'Reilly has been the golden boy of Irish business. In 1979, after a meteoric rise through the company ranks, O'Reilly became chief executive of the Heinz corporation, based in Pittsburgh. He stepped down from that post in the spring of 1998, but remains chairman of the company.

Immensely wealthy, highly intelligent and very charming, he has played personal host to South African President Nelson Mandela, played golf with at least one US President, counts the famous former editor of the *Washington Post* – Ben Bradlee – among his international board members, and divorced his first wife and mother of his six children to marry multi-millionairess Chryss Goulandris, a member of one of the most prominent Greek shipping families and one of the late Christina Onassis's best friends.

In 1973, O'Reilly bought control of Independent Newspapers in Dublin for just one million pounds. That company now has assets of five hundred million pounds and effectively controls businesses worth a billion.[2]

Since the beginning of 1994, the Independent group has acquired 60 per cent of the Argus group, South Africa's largest newspaper chain; 55 per cent of Australian Provincial Newspapers; 25 per cent of Irish Press Newspapers in Ireland; and 44 per cent of Wilson and Horton, the largest newspaper group in New Zealand. It also has extensive interests in cable television in Ireland; radio and television in Australia; and outdoor advertising in Portugal, France and Mexico. In March 1998, O'Reilly achieved his long-held ambition of owning a British broadsheet, when he assumed full control of the daily *Independent* – a newspaper he has reportedly referred to as 'my finest calling card'.

O'Reilly's long-term and frequently thwarted pursuit of a status-symbol newspaper title came in for much media analysis. His Irish titles were immensely successful, providing the bedrock for many of his later international acquisitions, but none of them provided the international media cachet that O'Reilly seemed rather desperately to want.

When the news broke of O'Reilly's intended outright buy of the British *Independent* titles, one media analyst was quoted as saying, 'It looks like vanity publishing. The [British] *Independent* will find it hard to make money, but a national newspaper still provides a platform for an ambitious man.'[3]

The *Sunday Times* journalist Matthew Lynn commented in the same edition, 'That O'Reilly is a vain man there is little doubt: his newspapers around the world are often filled with stories about himself, in language so flowery even [Robert] Maxwell might have blushed. "He sits astride the world with more ease and panache than most world leaders," wrote

2 It is estimated to control 70 per cent of the Irish newspaper market. In April 1998, Independent Newspapers recorded £100.1 million pre-tax profits.
3 *Sunday Times*, March 8 1998.

Ireland's *Sunday Independent* some years ago. "He is a gifted human being." '

O'Reilly's pursuit of a trophy title was probably influenced by his friendship with Ben Bradlee, the man who presided over the historic Watergate affair. O'Reilly was a member of the *Washington Post* board.

In Bradlee's recent autobiography, *A Good Life*, the relationship between the two men is noted, and the mutual admiration is obvious. Commenting on his post-retirement activities, Bradlee writes:

> All that plus writing this book had pretty much filled up my dance card when the charismatic Dr Anthony John Francis O'Reilly made me an offer I couldn't refuse. With one hat, Tony O'Reilly is the chairman and CEO of the multi-billion-dollar H.J. Heinz Co. I knew him as a fellow *Washington Post* board member . . . . With another hat, O'Reilly runs his own media company – and I'm on his board – with major newspapers in Ireland and South Africa, nearly half of the *Independent* in London, plus newspapers and radio stations and outdoor advertising in Australia and a smaller share of the largest newspaper in New Zealand.

In Ireland, O'Reilly had been a dominant and influential figure for decades. In private, Irish politicians may carp and criticise the great man; in public they bow the knee and doff the cap. On the one known occasion they did not – in 1997, when the government refused to do the group's bidding in relation to a commercial broadcasting matter – a leaked memo suggested that the government had been told by Independent representatives that it was about to lose the 'friendship' of the group.

The memo was leaked after the daily newspaper, *Irish Independent* had urged its readers to vote for the opposition parties in that year's general election – an unusual move in Irish journalism and one which enraged the governing parties, who promptly lost that election.

The Independent group denied that the 'spin' on the memo's contents was accurate; the 'loss of friendship', it said, referred to the difficulties the group might now face in preventing its commercial partners from taking court action on the issue.

The allegation made by the government was impossible to prove either way. Shortly afterwards, *Irish Times* journalist John Waters, a long-time *Sunday Independent* 'victim' and one of the group's most trenchant critics, wrote:

> When you lose the friendship of the Independent group, a number of symptoms manifest themselves with speed. As though by some miraculous process, several journalists working for Independent Newspapers suddenly and simultaneously become fascinated by your every move and utterance.
>
> A single edition of one of the group's newspapers will contain several articles dealing with aspects of your life and opinions, all either violently hostile, mocking or dismissive. To the degree that your professional life depends on the oxygen of good publicity in Independent-controlled newspapers, you are doomed to suffocate. Politicians, knowing the worth of every vote, are most vulnerable to this.

Waters argued that Dr A.J.F. O'Reilly's power was such that he had no need to keep in constant contact with his newspapers in order to have them print the items that pleased him and omit any stories that might upset him.

Instead, Waters argued, O'Reilly's policy was one of cultivating key journalists, with a view to ensuring that his flagship columns remained in keeping with the overall design and 'façade of independence'. These journalists were highly paid, in most cases, but on short-term contracts, an arrangement that ensured the maximum loyalty. 'It is remarkable how often journalists who work for the Independent group feel it necessary to assure all and sundry that they have never been told what to write. I don't doubt it. They already know what they are expected to write.'

Waters repeated much of this – and worse – on the *Questions and Answers* TV programme on RTE one night. He described the newspaper as 'vile' and criticised the then government's failure to do something about O'Reilly's monopoly in the Irish newspaper market.

Later he recalled how none of the politicians on the panel with him dared to support his view:

> It was a bit like smoking behind the school shed and all the others giggling at you for being so daring. Here were these politicians wondering, 'Oh, my God, what will the *Sunday Independent* do to us? We'd better keep quiet.' And afterwards they said to me, 'You're for it now.' These people, who had the power to do something about the man, were leaving it to me and then telling me that I would be for it. And I did get it; I got it for a full year and a half after that.

Another peculiarity of the *Sunday Independent* – and critical to the story of Veronica Guerin's death – is the manner in which it personalises its own reporting staff. Over time, and particularly during the early 1990s, certain journalists adopted the personae of characters in a bizarre journalistic soap opera.

One of them – Barry Egan – became the rakish 'man about town', interviewing Dublin's prettiest women – relentless weekly encounters involving a great deal of alcohol and photographs to challenge even the most outrageous victim's modesty.

'She drinks Bollinger like it was her birthright – and white wine too,' he wrote about one such woman; another was described as having 'alcohol trickling through her veins . . .'

The editor defended Egan's words on the grounds that his son's teenage friends enjoyed his column.

The real lives of the journalists on the paper started to be packaged and sold. They now write about their love affairs, the births of their children, the deaths of parents, their sex lives, their neuroses, their underwear; nothing is too personal to be recounted. They go on diets, have colonic irrigations, and write about it, they have mud wraps and not only write about it but allow themselves to be photographed as well.

Madeleine Keane – daughter of Terry Keane, the paper's gossip columnist – wrote a harrowing account of how her own daughter had swallowed sleeping tablets and survived. Every snippet of staff trauma has entered the public domain.

Many of the persuaded have been young, still in their twenties – a willing pool of confessors who can hardly complain about their privacy being invaded. If outside personalities cannot be cajoled into telling all, the *Sunday Independent* has the perfect solution: they grow their own.

When Veronica died, and few journalists would even whisper this, the paper found itself in possession of the biggest Irish news story in decades, and one which touched all the *Sunday Independent* editorial buttons.

The main figure was a young attractive woman, the murdered mother of a young child. Central to the story was the lurid, fascinating world of organised crime and, over-riding even this, it was one of the paper's own journalists that had died.

Veronica could not write her own epitaph, but at least her husband could be persuaded to put pen to paper – which he did – as well as appearing with his son in countless photographs.

The bedrock of the features section of the paper – some would argue the bedrock of the entire paper – was and is the Terry Keane column. This is ostensibly a gossip column in the traditional mode, but made even more titillating by Keane's incessant, coy references to her long-standing relationship with the former Taoiseach, Charles Haughey – column after column peppered with *doubles entendres* about the man she calls 'sweetie'.

She has hinted at foreign hotels they have stayed in; sojourns she had enjoyed on his island, on his yacht, the quality of the sex and, when Haughey was still in power, she suggested that she was privy to some of his decision-making.

Elsewhere she provides the usual gossip column staples of openings, parties, marital break-ups, engagements, alleged affairs. The column was and is wittily put together. It has been reported that the column is in fact a *mélange* of contributions edited, not by Keane, but rather by the paper's powerful deputy editor, Anne Harris. This has neither been confirmed nor denied.

Much of the newspaper's editorial borders on the salacious; those people brave enough to criticise its tone and content are mocked, often viciously, dismissed as 'establishment' drones who, clinging to outmoded 'politically correct' values, are not in touch with the real views of the people. These 'real views' are presumably scientifically ascertained by the *Independent* through copious amounts of market research.

Its most controversial and marketable columnist – apart from Keane – was former soccer player Eamon Dunphy. Dunphy specialised in contrarianism. He particularly specialised in biting the ankles of anyone he judged to be a member of 'Official Ireland' – an eclectic mix of people ranging variously from cabinet ministers to *Irish Times* columnists.

Dunphy's private *alter ego*, nonetheless, has counted among his friends some of 'Official Ireland's most prominent, not to mention richest, icons', including former government press secretary, P.J. Mara, Paul McGuinness, manager of U2, and a variety of names that graced the gossip columns. Dunphy was also an *habitué* of the Shelbourne Hotel bar – a virtual home-from-home for the denizens of Official Ireland.

But Dunphy was a great acquisition by the *Sunday Independent*. He is a very gifted writer and has written critically acclaimed and commercially successful non-fiction, notably his biography of U2. But it was his wilder moments that were most applauded by his editors, whose only known directive to their star was that he be 'passionate'.

When Dunphy, in 1992, called the former Tánaiste Dick Spring a 'bollocks of the highest order', Aengus Fanning commented that Dunphy was 'breaking new ground . . . it was expressing something in the vernacular, in language in daily use. I instinctively went with it. I knew what he was doing: it was giving the paper that chemistry I talked about earlier.'

Curiously Dunphy has admitted – in 1997, as a defendant

in a libel action taken by then cabinet minister Proinsias De Rossa – that at least some of his views should not be taken too seriously.[4] He noted that many of his 'victims' had either gone on to greater things or were more loved than ever by the public. In attempting to play down the impact of the alleged libel, Dunphy has debunked himself.

The *Sunday Independent* spectacularly lost the libel action some months later – De Rossa was awarded record damages. That night, it was later reported, Tony O'Reilly's son, Gavin, took Dunphy out to dinner.

By this stage Dunphy had also fallen out with his *Sunday Independent* employers. He had transferred his contrarianism to Radio Ireland (now Today FM). The reasons why he left, as this book will reveal, were intimately linked to the death of Veronica Guerin.

Irish Times journalist John Waters worked for the *Sunday Independent* for a brief period in the late 1980s. Since then, he has had a highly successful career as a writer and an *Irish Times* columnist. He has been a regular target for the *Sunday Independent* and he in turn has attacked the ethos of the paper and its media monopoly in Ireland. In late 1997 he was awarded significant damages from the *Sunday Independent* in settlement of an action taken by Waters over an article by Eamon Dunphy in 1995.[5] In a published apology, the newspaper acknowledged that the comments made in Dunphy's article were 'based upon untruths about his [Waters's] personal conduct.'

4 Dunphy had claimed that De Rossa had tolerated and even supported some of the harsher elements of the old communist regime in Russia. De Rossa is leader of Democratic Left, a moderately left-wing party, which had evolved from a split with Sinn Féin in the 1970s. During the 1970s and early 1980s, it would have supported some communist regimes, but it had moved very far away from that type of ideology by the time it entered government with the centre-right Fine Gael party and the Labour Party in 1994.

5 Dunphy wrote an article, published in the *Sunday Independent* on May 7 1995, which was mostly an attack on Waters for his own recent attack on Tony O'Reilly and Independent Newspapers. But Dunphy also claimed that he had once given Waters a gift of £1,000 and arranged a job for him on the *Sunday Independent*. The money claim was at the core of Waters's libel case.

In 1996, Waters and singer Sinead O'Connor had a baby daughter, an event which gave rise to more sneering comment from the *Sunday Independent*, notably in the Terry Keane column.

The next chapter records his memory of the *Sunday Independent* as a contributor and his view of the newspaper from the outside. He is, objectively, a hostile witness, but his is a voice that has won respect through his columns in *The Irish Times* and through his other work. It deserves attention.

7

GOODIES AND BADDIES

'I would prefer to be at the mercy of the British tabloid press than at the mercy of the *Sunday Independent*.'

John Waters

'The sales of the paper are amazing,' Waters told me. 'It's sold on the basis of sleaze and titillation and sensation and abuse and invective. What they've done is turn all these things into commodities which have become highly saleable.'

Waters stopped buying the paper some time ago, but admits that this makes him feel unusual. On any Sunday, in any given public place, copies of the *Sunday Independent* are ubiquitous – everyone seems to be reading it.

But, says Waters, a vast proportion of people claim to be nauseated by the paper's content and style. A huge contradiction, certainly, if a profitable one. And there is apparently nothing particularly complex about this success.

Waters worked for the paper for six months, from the end of 1988 to the summer of 1989, and very quickly he understood the principle upon which it operated:

On the basis of two lists of people. Everybody in the world was divided into two lists; you were either a goodie in the *Independent*'s terms, or you were a baddie, and every word in the paper had to . . . reflect this.

So if I were to write about somebody, I would first of all have to know what list they were on, and I would have to treat them appropriately. Nobody tells you to do so, you just breathe it in . . .

One of the first things Waters noticed was the very different way in which the *Sunday Independent* operated. In the fast-moving world of national newspapers, the average young journalist has around seven-and-a-half minutes at conference to make his or her case to the editor, but in the *Sunday Independent*, the opposite seemed to be the case. Editors, says Waters, 'had no end of time for you, to talk to you and make you feel that they were your friends and that you were being invited to join a family. They flattered you and made you feel really good about yourself.'

The flattery and attention encouraged the journalists to want to belong to the editorial team and to support the editorial line.

'Aengus Fanning was a very eccentric character, very funny and kind of philosophical. You'd go in for chats and you'd end up talking about everything except what you were supposed to be talking about. He'd be asking you what you thought of this and that and it was . . . like they were vetting your views.'

But these views with which the editor was so concerned had little to do with the salient issues of the day, the big political stories about Northern Ireland, or the Middle East.

'I remember one occasion early on. I was also writing for the *Evening Herald* and I wrote about a particular individual in that paper – the TV presenter Bibi Baskin. I made a cheap joke about her and Anne Harris rang me up and asked me did I not understand that Bibi Baskin was someone who should be supported and who was a great talent and who deserved to be treated properly. I'd actually got her on the wrong list.'

Until then, Waters had never seen the world in terms of lists. But he rapidly realised that, if he wanted to keep his job, he would have to. 'If I was writing about [a well-known nationalist activist], I would have to know that the correct designation for this person was "Provo sympathiser, anarchist, trouble-maker". That was his role in the world as defined by the *Sunday Independent*. I had to make that clear; I could never write about him as the witty and trenchant commentator that he is.'

61

The consequence of a foul-up, i.e. writing something on the basis of your own views and against the *Sunday Independent* line, would be exile. 'The phone calls would dry up for a few days, maybe for a week or so. You wouldn't be getting the invitation to write more stuff.'

Very different from the reaction when a story reflecting the *Sunday Independent* line had gone down well. 'The phone would ring first thing on Tuesday morning and it would be congratulations and commissions to beat the band.'

Adopting the *Sunday Independent*'s particular view of the world had very seductive benefits. 'Once I internalised it, then I could make a lot of money and gain notoriety and fame and celebrity.'

Psychologically, it was easy to become hooked. Journalism is a demanding, lonely and often thankless task. 'No other newspaper supports you. You get no support morally or emotionally. You get paid and that's it. The *Sunday Independent* supports you in every way. They treat you as if you are playing a game; they treat you as a hero . . . someone who is absolutely one of them.'

The support that *Sunday Independent* journalists come to rely on is the polar opposite of the powerlessness felt by its many victims.

> If you're working for the *Sunday Independent* and somebody writes about you and calls you a gobshite, the *Sunday Independent* will ring you up and comfort you and tell you you're great and that the person who wrote about you is only a bollocks and why don't you come out and have a cup of coffee? In any other paper . . . the senior management would go round the place wondering why they had a gobshite working for them.

The management had skilfully created a context within which they could rely on their journalists to contribute to their agenda, without necessarily having to force them. Everybody craves approval. And once any reasonably intelligent and versatile person has learnt how to earn that approval, of course they will continue to do the 'right' thing.

Veronica Guerin, Waters believes, was attractive to the *Sunday Independent* because of the shock waves created by the Bishop Casey story, which she wrote while she was working on the *Sunday Tribune*. 'When you made any sort of ripple at all, they wanted to employ you and of course they could afford to pay you if you did the business for them. In a way it was inevitable that anybody would end up working for them.'

Even though Veronica Guerin had forged a reputation as an intuitive and uncompromising journalist, the *Sunday Independent*, says Waters, was never particularly interested in journalism as such. The average story say, for instance, the causes and aftermath of flash floods in western Ireland, which might take several days to research and write – would be rewarded with a derisory sum and given an insignificant amount of space.

'Now if I stayed at home and waited for Anne Harris to ring me and Anne had somebody who was in their sights that week; Sinead O'Connor or Chris De Burgh or Van Morrison or anybody – and I decided to do a thousand words of rant about it, I'd sit down and set the clock and start to write.'

Writing against the clock became a curious feature of *Sunday Independent* internal culture. 'One particular guy told me he used to have a fetish that each week he would try to get more money for spending less time working for the *Sunday Independent*.' It is not hard, Waters says, to see this as the consequences of a troubled conscience. 'The only way he could morally justify what he was doing was to . . . cheat them in some metaphysical sense.'

Bizarrely enough, it was very easy to get away with it. 'If you wrote your thousand words of rant in fifty minutes, without any reference to documents or clippings, without talking to anybody, and then sent it in, you would be published . . . given half a page with a cartoon of the individual you were writing about; it might be flagged on the front and you would receive calls from Aengus and Anne within hours of when it came out and you'd be a star and you'd probably get five hundred pounds for it.'

Waters found out very quickly that traditional journalism didn't pay in the *Sunday Independent*, not merely in terms of the length of time you put in to your stories, but also in terms of the unstated pressure, from week to week, to go one step further, earn higher accolades from your employers. 'If you look at somebody like Eamon Dunphy, Dunphy had to constantly up the ante in terms of being trenchant and in terms of his invective. If you called somebody a bollocks this week, you'd have to call them a fucking bollocks the next.'

Waters' view of the *Sunday Independent* was not an isolated one. The paper's unique selling point for a lengthy period was the extraordinary nature of its weekly polemics, both in terms of volume and scattergun vitriol.

Nevertheless, the newspaper did occasionally produce ground-breaking scoops. In 1993 reporter Sam Smyth won the Journalist of the Year award for his investigative work. In later years, journalists, including Veronica Guerin, Rory Godson and Jody Corcoran, helped to develop the investigative news side of the paper.

Yet in an interview with Aengus Fanning by Ivor Kenny in his book *Talking to Ourselves*, Fanning himself admitted that news was not a priority for the *Sunday Independent*. He said: 'There is no staple diet of news on a Saturday. The *Sunday Independent* . . . is a magazine wrapped up in a newspaper. News still has a place in the scheme of things, but what I have consciously gone for is more of a magazine. If people are as bored on Sunday as they say they are, they need entertainment, they need a talking point, something to provoke and stimulate.'

But, as we shall demonstrate in the next chapter, stimulation was only one element of what the *Sunday Independent* provided. Strong evidence from another key figure in the *Sunday Independent* suggests that the selection of targets was far from arbitrary.

8

A CURIOUS BEAST

Fintan O'Toole is another habitué of the *Sunday Independent* hit list. Like Waters, he is an *Irish Times* columnist and author – arguably one of the best and most respected journalists of his generation. In July 1997, he and his family left for New York for a year, after O'Toole had taken leave of absence to become a drama critic for the *Daily News*.

He has frequently written about Tony O'Reilly and Independent Newspapers, most recently in the Spring 1996 edition of *Granta* magazine, in an article entitled 'Brand Leader'.

Eamon Dunphy has regularly had O'Toole in his sights, once boasting that he had rung O'Toole and told him that he was going 'to get' him. Critics point out that O'Toole shows a tendency to become over-passionate when sounding off about his own *bêtes noires*. Nevertheless, the cornerstone of much of O'Toole's writing is a humanity, an honesty, a rigorous approach to the truth – as he sees it – and above all a basic decency.

None of this has endeared him to the editorial élite of the *Sunday Independent*. Like Waters, he too is a hostile witness; like Waters, his views are also worthy of consideration.

O'Toole considers the *Sunday Independent* to be an extraordinary editorial creation, a 'cross between the *Spectator* and the *Sun*'. At its core, he says, is a body of opinionated pieces, written generally by the same people and broadly arguing from a position which is rightwing in economic terms, antinationalist in terms of Northern Ireland and supportive of the

65

interests of the *Sunday Independent* and its owner.

'The most spectacular example of that was in relation to the exploration for oil off the south coast of Ireland in the late seventies and early eighties.'

> That was a period when oil shares were driven by media perception of how likely it was that there was going to be a find. There was no doubt about the fact that the hysteria was fed partly by the Irish Independent group, whether that's coincidental or not is hard to say, but it was certainly the case.
>
> And at any time that there's been an attack on either the *Sunday Independent* or the Independent Group or O'Reilly, those attacks have had to be made in the certain knowledge that there would be retribution and that the retribution would be . . . nuclear.[1]

That core is dressed in something more glittery – ideological still, but softer. 'It's about selling a certain idea of lifestyle, a certain idea of fun, a certain idea of what a contemporary Irish person ought to be like.' O'Toole calls this element 'post-Catholic'. Promoting a culture of hedonism, where beautiful people have affairs and dark, interesting private lives.

The *Sunday Independent*, for O'Toole, is a heady brew of these two elements: 'the promotion of a sort of Irish aristocracy on the one hand and the promotion of a very specific and clear ideological agenda on the other'.

O'Toole points out that the *Independent*'s ideological agenda is apparent from the politics of those it victimises.

> The overwhelming criterion . . . has tended . . . to be people who fall foul of a very clear ideological line on Northern Ireland, and undoubtedly the most spectacular example of a victim pursued with relentless vigour was the SDLP leader John Hume, when he was beginning what subsequently

1 Tony O'Reilly had a personal interest in the subject through his control of Atlantic Resources, an oil exploration company.

became known as 'the peace process' and when he was beginning to soften his approach to Gerry Adams and Sinn Féin. To pursue the idea of the pan-nationalist front.

It is, of course, reasonable to expect a newspaper to take a stand on certain issues. But, according to O'Toole, the *Sunday Independent* was truly remarkable for the ferocity with which it put forward its views. 'What was extraordinary was the extent and the persistence of it. Instead of having one piece, or two pieces, which were arguing against a certain line, you would have a bombardment, and you would have a dramatisation of people as the enemy. Hume was chosen as the enemy at one particular point.'

The paper had plenty of 'enemies'. The Labour Party was certainly targeted after it came to power (in 1992), and after its coalition with Fianna Fáil. Fianna Fáil itself became an enemy, partly because of its stance on Northern Ireland. But also because it had fallen outside of the 'consensus Ireland' that the *Sunday Independent* saw itself as representing. 'The new consensus of a post-nationalist, secular society.'

What was so astonishing for O'Toole was the lack of balance. In almost all other papers, and with the presentation of news on TV and radio, he argues, 'there's at least a perception that what's going on is investigative journalism, that you're finding things out and presenting them to the public'. In the *Sunday Independent*, O'Toole did not even detect a pretence at this. No attempt to stress that its judgements were individual and 'independent' – one side of a wider debate.

There was undoubtedly a sense that certain people had been chosen to be victims and that once they had been chosen, there was nothing they could do right. So it was journalism as a form of punishment, rather than journalism as a form of investigation. The newspaper almost saw itself as an organ of retribution for people who had stepped outside [the] line which the *Sunday Independent* had decided upon.

Not that people couldn't cross those lines. O'Toole

describes himself as having once been 'a darling figure' for the *Sunday Independent*, and then, after having written a critical piece about the *Sunday Independent* in relation to a particular story, he found he had crossed the lines overnight. 'No further flattering references . . . any reference would necessarily be hostile . . . '

O'Toole, describing himself as 'a very boring and conservative individual', was lucky to have escaped any salacious uprooting of his private life. Others were not so lucky.

'A very good example was a long attack on Brendan Howlin[2] over something which was not terribly important. It was a political issue, but the criticism was all about him being not a very tall man.'

The *Sunday Independent* saw no problem in attacking its enemies, not on the basis of their beliefs or views, but upon purely arbitrary, personal criteria.

'Michael D. Higgins was another favourite target at different points.[3] Consistently attacked not only for what he was saying or doing but also because of his voice, because of his personal idiosyncrasies . . .'

This, then, was the peculiar adversarial atmosphere into which Veronica Guerin came. The *Sunday Independent*, a publication which saw the need for enemies, created them, identified them, and exposed them.

The *Sunday Independent*'s staff were, as we have seen, key players in the theatrical atmosphere it created. The editor famously allowed himself to be photographed swimming with one of his then regular contributors, Sineve Soe.

Editorial policy was, says O'Toole, directed at creating a spectacle closer to TV than a newspaper. 'Instead of somebody coming in and telling you, "This is the Bosnian situation," it was like a chat show where someone would sit down and ask, "How did you get there?" and "What was it like for you?"'

2 Brendan Howlin is now deputy leader of the Labour Party, and was a government minister from 1992 to 1997.
3 A Labour Party TD and former government minister.

And in such a climate, the paper's ideological position, such as it was, went largely unstated. It was taken for granted that its enemies deserved to be attacked.

'Take the case of the attack on Courtney Kennedy [see Chapter 6], on her appearance. It's her own fault for having married someone who is ideologically suspect and really, if she has taken that step, then she is the enemy and once you're the enemy, then there are no rules any more.'

The *Sunday Independent* declined to co-operate with this book. I could have spoken to reporters whom I knew there, but there was little point if none of them would go on the record, or if their on-the-record interviews were going to be done with many a backward glance towards their bosses.

But I sensed that Eamon Dunphy would talk to me. By this stage, Dunphy had fallen out with the *Sunday Independent* for reasons which will be dealt with in a later chapter, although he was still very loyal to and friendly with editor Aengus Fanning.

In an earlier interview with the *Sunday Tribune*, Dunphy had expressed his frustration with certain elements of the paper's editorial policy, using the word 'cancer' at one point, to describe the ethos. *Sunday Independent* reporters later came to describe one part of the office as the 'cancer ward'.

Dunphy was by now presenting the increasingly controversial and successful *Last Word* programme on the country's new national station Radio Ireland. We met in a nearby hotel for the interview, Dunphy chain-smoking throughout, drinking only mineral water. It became clear that Veronica's death had disturbed him greatly. It also became clear that he was frustrated at what he believed was a media misunderstanding of the complex nature of the paper he once wrote for and became almost synonymous with.

The *Sunday Independent*, he believes, is really two newspapers wrapped in one. He wrote for one of those newspapers, while Terry Keane and the other lifestyle and feature columnists wrote for the other. The only problem with the paper, he says, is that, after a while people failed to distinguish between the two.

Dunphy had come to work for the *Sunday Independent* under Aengus Fanning, shortly after Fanning had become editor. Previously he had worked under Vincent Browne on the *Sunday Tribune*, where his trenchant opinions and no-prisoners-taken analysis of sport, and particularly soccer, had marked him out from the rest of his colleagues in sports journalism.

But on the *Sunday Independent* his brief was widened. He wrote on sport, he had a television column and, within a short period of time, he secured the back page of the news section to write on anything he liked – from politics to popular culture.

Fanning at the time was also recruiting a number of other contract contributors, including journalist and novelist Colm Tóibín; author, historian and sometime government adviser on the arts, Anthony Cronin; journalist John Waters for a brief period; stockbroker and senator Shane Ross, historian Ronan Fanning; and a number of others. All were respected writers, all had strong opinions on virtually everything. Over time, they came to dominate the newspaper, while many of the long-serving staff reporters barely got a look in.

Like most of the non-staff contributors, Dunphy worked from home, regularly discussing with Fanning the future direction of the paper. He speaks with great respect for his former boss. 'Fanning's great quality as an editor was that he was brave; he supported you. I was writing deeply unpopular stuff, especially about John Hume and the SDLP, and he was running it. I had been writing revisionist stuff about John Hume since my time on the *Tribune*. Hume had been a particular target of mine since the mid-eighties.

'Aengus just wanted good writing; he didn't care about the politics. The dominant political view was revisionist, was anti-nationalist.' Dunphy told me that, until recently, he had been unaware that a branch of Fanning's family was Protestant and Unionist. 'In terms of the North, there was never any concerted policy.'

So why then, were people whose attitudes were more conciliatory, or pro-nationalist, attacked? 'There may have been nine articles attacking Albert Reynolds one week, but that was just down to the whimsy of the individual columnists. You could criticise the editor for not balancing that, but in terms of nationalism, or revisionism, the paper never had a policy.'

Dunphy argues that the paper – his half of the hybrid, at least – was a forum for strong writers. It attracted them to its fold. 'After about three years, we were making an impact in terms of circulation. When we got myself and the other contributors together . . . the centre of intellectual gravity in journalism moved away from the *Sunday Tribune* and over to the *Sunday Independent*.'

The motives of Fanning and Dunphy were, he claims, very simple – to transform a paper that was tired and conventional to a paper that was alive and challenging. The hiring policy was based on the selection of good, original writers – 'the yardstick should be the originality and courage of the opinion, and the ability to deliver it in the language of journalism . . . '

Aengus Fanning not only achieved that, but supported his writers whenever the going got tough.

But then, in Dunphy's view, something began to happen to that challenging, thought-provoking side of the paper: it became eclipsed by its lighter, 'sexier' twin. The gossip, the scandal and the voyeuristic side began to take over. 'We had started to make an impact on circulation which was quite considerable and growing, but this [rumour] started to go around Independent House that it's the Terry Keane column that sells the paper.'

Keane's column had started in the late eighties. Aengus Fanning had once remarked to Dunphy that the paper's growing success came from a certain voyeuristic tendency, in rural Ireland particularly, which demanded to see the lives of the conspicuous laid bare.

Dunphy himself was uncertain. His gut instincts as a journalist told him that it was the sports section and the intellectual heavyweights such as Colm Tóibín that sold the paper. 'But this myth about the potency of the Terry Keane column took hold . . . '

Dunphy admits that it is hard for him to surmise on the validity of this conviction. He worked from home. He was hardly ever in the offices of the *Sunday Independent*. But nevertheless he saw the changes. And he deplored them.

In 1990, Dunphy registered a very serious protest when someone's private life was intruded into.

I said to Aengus; look this is a fucking monster. Our paper will be undermined as a serious newspaper. Seven, eight years ago I said that you can't trade in sleaze of this kind – the article on that Kennedy girl was a classic example. It was pernicious and ugly.

I knew an actress whose relationship split up and she was going through hell and it was traumatic for her. But the next thing she's on the back page with her photograph and it's treated as a joke, the fact that someone's life is wrecked. These weren't even important public figures.

Then there was this 'Living and Leisure' section where Mick Doyle and Terry Keane and Madeleine Keane would all go off to a hotel and be the glossy photograph on the front cover. It just wasn't right; journalists shouldn't do that. Now that 'tendency' *is* the paper and now it's an alien place for people who want to practise journalism.

Dunphy argues that this tendency became dominant because the editorial balance of power shifted to Anne Harris, who wanted to promote that kind of journalism.

Dunphy contends that his own attacks on public figures were legitimate in the public interest. The problem, he claims, was the confusion in the minds of people, including Fintan O'Toole, between Dunphy's polemics and the personal, invasive attacks written elsewhere in the *Sunday Independent*.

We [Dunphy and his 'side' of the paper] were hurting people like Seamus Heaney and Mary Robinson. They were hurtful, biting polemics about people who were prospering in a provincial country that had lost the run of itself.

But the thing that made people uneasy was the egregious

sleaze. Now that complaint – against sleaze – was legitimate, the other was not legitimate. Fintan O'Toole wrote a
piece [in *The Irish Times*] in which he detected the hand of
Eoghan Harris[4] in my work. It was a vicious piece about
Eoghan Harris's manipulation of the *Sunday Independent*
[suggesting that he influenced] what me and other people
were writing, which was a preposterous idea.

O'Toole's error, Dunphy claims, was to have misunder-
stood the paper's dual nature. And once people identified the
Sunday Independent solely with its scandalmongering,
personally abusive side, the reputation stuck.

John Waters swiftly followed with a piece in the *Irish Times*
entitled 'Tony O'Reilly's Evil Empire', and, according to
Dunphy, made the same error. His attack centred, not upon
the paper's more frivolous elements, but on the kind of pieces
that Dunphy wrote. He did not mention Dunphy by name,
but said that attacks on Seamus Heaney and the like had
debased Irish journalism.

'People can make their own minds up as to whether
polemics which do not deal in any way with people's personal
life are "evil".' I never write about people's personal lives; I
write about people in their public personae.'

Dunphy says that the black and white perception of the
Sunday Independent grew increasingly obvious. He uses the
example of the RTE TV programme *Questions and Answers*.
'Someone in the audience would just have to say something
pejorative about the paper and that was it – people would
applaud . . . frequently a panellist would use the *Sunday
Independent* as an exemplar of something dreadful.'

So gradually, Dunphy feels, the public's understanding of
what Fanning and himself had set out to do became obscured.
When the public thought about the paper, they thought only
of Terry Keane. 'But to believe that it was a homogeneous

4 A well-known polemicist and writer, Eoghan Harris is the separated husband
of *Sunday Independent* deputy editor, Anne Harris. He holds strongly anti-
republican views.

piece was very unfair to the good journalists who were in there.'

For a time, Dunphy stuck to his guns, continuing a 'polite discourse' with Aengus Fanning, and asking him to hire more strong, provocative writers, using the current success to get them on board. 'Because I knew that the other thing – the sleaze – was threatening to take the paper over and I felt increasingly that I was a kind of alien in there.'

It is, he argues, essential for a writer to feel proud of the paper he writes for. But this became increasingly hard. And his dissent did not pass unnoticed. 'I became a pain in the arse.'

9

ON THE BEAT

From Veronica's closest colleagues, as we have seen in the earlier chapters, a consistent picture was emerging. Of a dedicated, skilful reporter, whose commitment to her work set her apart from all other journalists, and whose enthusiasm bordered, at times, upon the ruthless. Up until the time she left the *Sunday Tribune*, her more reckless actions had been frowned upon, but failed to jeopardise her career or her safety.

However, when she moved to a paper which built its very reputation on derring-do, she put into action a chain of events which would eventually lead to her death. In January 1994, Veronica Guerin moved to the *Sunday Independent*.

Veronica Guerin's first story for the *Sunday Independent* was published on January 9 1994. By September she had nine front-page exclusive stories under her belt.

She had already published some crime stories in the *Sunday Business Post* and the *Sunday Tribune*, as detailed above, her biggest, in September 1993, being the story of the recovery of the Beit family paintings.

The story was told in great detail, clearly supplied by Gardaí sources, although one senior Garda, who later became a confidant of Veronica's, believed that by this stage Veronica had come into contact with John Traynor – a self-confessed and previously convicted fraudster – who would later emerge as her single biggest criminal contact.

It remains unclear whether the *Sunday Independent* expressly gave Veronica a brief to write about Dublin's underworld and the extent to which criminal gangs were controlling the city's mushrooming drug trade.

Writing in the *Sunday Independent* on October 20 1996, four months after Veronica's death, Anne Harris was at pains to stress that Veronica's brief was wider than crime. In an interview in the *Sunday Business Post* of October 17 1996, her brother Jimmy Guerin has also said that it annoyed her to be described as a crime reporter. She saw herself as an investigative reporter with a wide brief.

In a *Sunday Independent* interview, published in July 1996, after her death, Veronica stated that her involvement in crime reporting happened almost by accident.

Jim Lacey, manager of the National Irish Bank, had been kidnapped. Everybody knew who had done it, yet we were writing what the Gardaí were saying, and we decided in the *Sunday Independent* – look, who are these people, what will we do? The only way we are going to find out who they are is to talk to them. And it opened a new world to me.

The reference to the decision being made not just by Veronica but by her editors as well is interesting, given their later protestations that she did everything on her own initiative, bar physically slapping the ink on to the print rollers.

In terms of crime reporting, there was a gap in the market. Since the 1980s, crime journalists tended to rely on the Gardaí for virtually all their information, although there were exceptions. *Irish Times* journalists Seán Flynn and Padraig Yates had published *Smack* in the mid-1980s, a detailed and revealing examination of the heroin trade that was gripping Dublin.

The investigative magazine *Magill* had profiled the Dublin criminal known as The General, actually naming him as Martin Cahill. RTE's current affairs programme *Today Tonight* had also profiled him, memorably following him up a street while Cahill disguised himself in a children's mask.

But at the time of Veronica's recruitment to the *Sunday Independent*, the only other journalist writing consistently about gangland leaders and major drug dealers was Paul

Williams of the down-market, tabloid *Sunday World*, which was also part of the Independent stable. But the sensationalist brief he followed did not allow for further analysis or detail. Veronica and Williams would later compete exclusive-for-exclusive in this newly 'hot' field of organised crime.

Veronica's first story for the *Sunday Independent*, on January 9 1994, detailed a phone-tapping controversy involving the Gardaí anti-racketeering unit.

A number of non-crime-related stories followed, but in February she was back on the beat, this time with an interview with the widow of a man who had committed suicide, allegedly as a result of dealing with someone whom Veronica called 'a high-profile Dublin criminal'. She interviewed the man's wife, and a picture of his wife and children was also carried.

Two weeks later, Veronica produced her first major article on Dublin's gangland in a piece modestly entitled 'Organised Crime – The Truth'.

Most of Veronica's stories, in line with standard practice in the newspaper, were accompanied by a photo byline – a photograph of the author beside her name. The cult of personality overshadowed everything – including considerations of security. It never dawned on the *Sunday Independent* that, for someone poking around in an underworld awash with every kind of criminal from kidnappers and armed robbers, to murderers and pimps, some degree of anonymity was needed. Veronica was afforded the same in-your-face, star treatment as the gossip columnist.

The tone of the article was reasonably sober compared with what would come later. None of the criminals were named either directly or through the nicknames that would subsequently become commonly used, even to the point of parody.

She quoted Gardaí sources throughout the article, and they talk at length about one criminal in particular, easily identifiable to those in the know as the so-called General, Martin Cahill, who would be shot dead just a few months later in August 1994. This was the article which Veronica later said was sparked by her newspaper's interest in those behind the November 1993 kidnapping of Jim Lacey.

Two paragraphs stood out. Midway through the article she wrote: 'In the course of researching this article, the *Sunday Independent* spoke to both criminals and Gardaí. A number of suspected criminals, including "Dublin's most notorious", were asked to go on the record – all refused.'

Right from the start, Veronica was pushing out the boundaries of crime reporting – approaching criminals themselves and not relying, as the bulk of her colleagues did, on information from the Gardaí.

One week later, a follow-up article was published, this time headlined 'Ireland's Top 20 Criminals'. Once again, she had made direct approaches to several of these men, but at this stage, caution was still being exercised, whether by Veronica, the *Sunday Independent* editors, the lawyers, or all three.

She wrote that libel law prevented her from naming the men, but all their names were known to the *Sunday Independent* and to the Gardaí, and some had given interviews off the record. The criminals were simply listed A, B, C, etc.

Criminal A was quite clearly Martin Cahill, but his nickname was still not used. The rest were not identifiable to anyone outside the criminal fraternity. No details of their home addresses or workplaces were supplied; instead, the 'flavour' of their lives was conveyed through racy anecdote.

In April, quoting Gardaí sources, Veronica wrote about a passport fraud involving an anonymous 'Dublin criminal'. In May, she quoted from a confidential Gardaí briefing document, detailing alleged IRA involvement in a UK drugs racket.

During her first six months at the paper, Veronica wrote a significant number of crime articles. All were presented as 'major investigations', invariably with a picture byline and front-page blurb to attract readers inside. But she was also producing a number of sound financial and political stories, which again demonstrated her undeniable ability to secure inside information from many business and political institutions.

In March she wrote about 'beef baron' Larry Goodman's claim against the Rasheed bank in Iraq for an unpaid letter of credit from Saddam Hussein's government. That same month she wrote about a boardroom battle in the Woodchester Credit Lyonnais Bank.

Then, in May, she was back to Dublin's criminal heartland in a lengthy, two-part investigation – 'Deep in the Drugs Underworld'. The strap-line read: 'For this exclusive *Sunday Independent* two-part investigation, Veronica Guerin spoke to both the drug barons and the men who try to stop them. Her conclusions are disturbing.'

Personal detail was emphasised through the articles. 'He dresses in exorbitantly expensive Italian suits with flashy designer labels. His children are boarders in private schools. He takes his family on at least four holidays every year.'

The second part of the investigation began: 'At dead of night, sailing by radar alone, a yacht pulls into a rocky cove on the Cork coast. Its crew seem like holidaymakers. By the light of their torches you can see their sun-bronzed faces.'

It is unlikely that Veronica actually wrote many of these descriptive passages. A lot of her work was rewritten by journalist Stephen Dodd, who was blessed with an ability to put the *Sunday Independent* stamp on whatever Veronica produced. Curiously, it was Dodd who would write the bulk of the *Sunday Independent* articles about Veronica after her death. It was curious because Dodd himself admitted, in the *Sunday Independent* of June 22 1997, that he had only met the journalist once.

But Veronica's superb fact-gathering ability was evident throughout the reports. By this stage, it was clear that she was building up a significant dossier on the operations of the drug importers and dealers, and the identities of the main players.

She wrote that few of them risked prosecution, because it was their middle men, the drug couriers, who did the most dangerous work on behalf of the dealers. She also revealed the reluctance of the Revenue Commissioners to take on the more obviously wealthy criminals because they feared intimidation.

The strap-line made the claim that Veronica had spoken to the 'drugs barons', but the quotes from the alleged dealers themselves were skimpy. It was clear that the bulk of her information was still coming from the Gardaí.

There was, however, one conspicuous sentence in the May article, noteworthy because it marks the first time she dispensed with the distancing introduction: 'The *Sunday Independent* has . . . '

Instead she wrote: 'I was able to trace some of the dealers abroad.' From then on, it was the very personal 'I' that did everything. Veronica Guerin was about to become more than a hired journalist. She was about to become a player.

Throughout May and June Veronica was distracted from the criminal underworld by two particularly shocking murder cases. One was the death of Galway woman Philomena Gillane, stabbed when six months pregnant and dumped in a car boot in an Athlone car park. The other was the triple murder in County Clare of Imelda Riney, her three-year-old son Liam and Fr Joseph Walsh by Brendan O'Donnell.

When Veronica Guerin reported that Imelda Riney had been raped before her murder, she attracted strong criticism for revealing a particularly sordid twist on what was already a most distressing story. Nevertheless, everything she reported was later confirmed to be accurate.

Veronica also reported on the delay in identifying Riney's burnt-out car, found not long after Riney's disappearance, but not identified correctly 'due to a chassis mix-up'. This occurred, Veronica suggested, because the chassis number was barely legible after the fire damage.

The Gardaí had attracted heavy local criticism of their handling of the case, but Veronica allowed them to put their own side of the story. She wrote that

Gardaí in the area acknowledge their inability to co-ordinate information . . . they attribute the shortfall . . . to local Gardaí structures rather than inefficiency on the part of individual Gardaí . . . Gardaí would like to point out that between them and locals there is already a strained relationship in the area . . . Gardaí are strict on licensing laws . . . Gardaí from outside the area investigating the tragedy feel this may be why local Gardaí were not notified about certain events pertaining to the disappearance of Imelda and Liam Riney . . . till too late.

These were very controversial claims by the Gardaí. In effect they were blaming local people for delays in the investigation, delays which may have led to the failure to find Imelda and her son until it was too late. The faithful recording of their views might have been a quid pro quo, recompense for the inside information they had given Veronica about the triple murder – a not-unheard-of journalistic tactic.

But in the months to come Veronica would start to use this tactic with the criminals themselves – allowing them to spin their lines and settle their scores in her reports, in exchange for interviews. When she started to use this method, and was not stopped, she began to head down a very dangerous road.

In August 1994, an event took place which would have a seismic effect not just on the criminal underworld in Dublin and elsewhere, but also on crime reporting itself. That event was the killing of Martin Cahill, the so-called General, shot dead in broad daylight in the Dublin suburb of Ranelagh.

Cahill's murder had been preceded by three gangland killings, all of which Veronica had reported; her sources in each case were the Gardaí.

The murder of Cahill now gave her the opportunity to report on everything she knew about the dead man – whom it was now of course safe to name and impossible to libel. She also detailed her attempts to secure an interview with him over a lengthy period earlier in the year. Her account gave a very graphic insight into the obsessive way she operated.

The nature of her reporting was also changing. Gone were the straight accounts of criminals and what they did. Instead the focus, as it would be from this point on, was on how Veronica, the female crime reporter, interacted with the 'godfathers' of crime. The strap-line of the article on Cahill read: 'Veronica Guerin met Martin Cahill four times as she researched an article on the Dublin underworld. Though he never owned up to being The General, he talked to her about the Beit paintings job, his run-ins with the Gardaí and [his] rule of fear amongst the capital's criminal classes.'

Her opening paragraph read:

In January of this year, while researching a story on Dublin's criminal underworld, I first met Martin Cahill. *After six weeks of daily hand-delivered correspondence to his two Dublin homes, he finally began to talk to me* [my italics] . . . over an eighty-day period I met him four times . . . he agreed to talk of what he had heard on the street and suggested people to whom I could speak . . .

In agreeing to talk on his terms, I was aware that Cahill was playing the same games with me as he was with the Gardaí. He was in control of all our conversations and, because I needed access to his information and associates, I complied. I was conscious of the fact that, if I angered him, the talks would end.

A number of people whom I spoke to in researching this book suggested that the manner in which Veronica Guerin approached her subjects was not just combative, but deliberately abrasive, even abusive at times. Colleagues admired her tenacity, found it unique, but nevertheless, they agree that she harried her prey, or to use Rory Godson's term, she 'abraded' people in order to get them to talk. Doing that with 'ordinary' interviewees was perhaps unattractive. Doing it with known killers was highly dangerous.

That she used this technique with Cahill is evident from her article. She admits to having in effect forced him to talk to her through the simple expedient of turning up on his doorstep every single day for six weeks, and, as she had admitted in an earlier article, sometimes twice a day.

In this article, she taunted him about a less-than-successful kidnapping attempt involving businessman Jim Lacey and his family. She wrote: 'I put it to Cahill that really the kidnap had been badly planned, as it involved a lot of time and manpower for a small return. He glared at me and, speaking slowly, said, "But the cops look like fools again." He added that whoever was playing games with the Gardaí was winning, [and] that was worth everything.'

Despite the 'glare', Veronica wrote that she wasn't intimidated by Cahill and went on to recount a number of amusing anecdotes he had told her about his run-ins with the Gardaí.

Yet Veronica had good reason to be intimidated even if, as she claimed, she wasn't. Further down the article, she wrote this about the man whom she had tormented for six weeks in order to get him to talk.

I had been told by criminals and Gardaí of two particularly vicious crimes carried out by Martin Cahill. One of these crimes involved a suspected tout.[1] Cahill had taken his victim to a disused flat in the Hollyfield corporation flat complex in Rathmines and nailed him to the wooden floor. The Gardaí knew Cahill had personally carried out this crime, but the victim refused to confirm it had happened.

The other incident involved a former associate also suspected of touting. This victim was treated in equally harsh fashion. He was bundled into a van, taken to the Phoenix Park and ordered to strip semi-naked. Cahill put a knife to the victim's left thigh and began peeling off the skin down to his knees. This excruciating torture continued for more than an hour. The victim was then dumped unceremoniously in a side street off Rathmines, a Dublin suburb.

When I asked Cahill about these incidents, he was momentarily silent. Then, without any apparent emotion, he said he had heard nothing about them. He added that he considered such action fair treatment of anybody who would talk to the Gardaí.

I asked why he could not think of a more humane method of punishment. He replied that people remember pain and, when they think of talking, they'll remember that pain and won't talk. A bullet, he said, laughing, would be wasted on a tout. 'It's short and sweet, torture is long and painful.'

1 Police informer.

But whatever the dangers she had risked in the extra-ordinary manner in which she had approached Cahill, Veronica was safe at least in her post-mortem account of what Cahill had said to her. In her earlier investigations, before Cahill's death, she had talked about him in a very circumspect way and had not reported any of her conversations. Dead criminals, after all, cannot come after you.

But Veronica reported something else on that day. It was in a gossipy side-bar to the main report, but it was an item which nonetheless would later, reportedly, have major repercussions for the journalist.

Under the heading 'Brutality of a Family Man', Veronica outlined details of Cahill's personal relationships. Cahill, she wrote, had fathered nine children by two women – his wife, Frances, and her sister Tina. Both women, according to Veronica Guerin, had accepted this and Cahill had spent the last years of his life commuting the few hundred yards' distance between the two women's homes.

From where had Veronica acquired information like this, which was far outside the 'normal' bounds of conventional crime reporting? It was almost certainly known to the police who had kept Cahill under surveillance for years, but to whom else? The clue to Veronica's informant lay in the last few paragraphs.

She wrote: 'Cahill did have one fetish that an associate of his disclosed to the *Sunday Independent* this week. He loved watching blue movies and striptease shows. He went to elaborate lengths to go to various massage parlours in Dublin. According to his associate, he never engaged in sexual activity but was turned on by the girl stripping in front of him and walking naked around the room.'

This was dangerous stuff. To most readers it was just typical *Sunday Independent* froth – a dash of sex and voyeurism thrown in to spice up an otherwise straightforward article about a criminal, the sort of salacious gossip beloved of the newspaper.

But it was significant for two reasons. It showed that Veronica now had an obviously rewarding relationship with an 'associate' – and presumably a criminal associate – of one of the biggest-known underworld figures in the country in recent years. Perhaps this person was one of those to whom Cahill himself had suggested Veronica should talk.

It also showed that this person was willing to peddle damaging gossip about his now-dead associate, gossip that could, and did, anger the remaining members of Cahill's gang and also Cahill's close and extensive family network. Martin was dead, but Frances, Tina and the rest were still very much alive.

One week later, Veronica wrote another seminal piece. She was back on the Cahill story, this time reporting that Cahill's murder had been carried out by the IRA working through a Dublin north inner-city criminal gang. She stated that Cahill had angered the IRA when he allegedly dealt with Loyalist gangs in disposing of the stolen Beit paintings (see page 42).

The IRA's involvement was hardly news. They had already claimed the killing and the Gardaí appeared to believe the claim. But the news of the alleged involvement of the Dublin gang was dynamite. Few readers would have been aware of whom Veronica was talking. But criminals knew and the Gardaí knew. The man at whom she was pointing the finger was a criminal who would later be tagged by Veronica and others with the nickname 'The Monk'. In this piece she had neither identified him by name or nickname, but the detail she did supply was sufficient. She might as well have put his name in lights.

There was one other person who knew the man to whom Veronica was referring. That person was a TD for the Dublin Central constituency. The Monk was a constituent. The TD's name was Tony Gregory and, from the first time he noticed Veronica's work, he became afraid for her safety and that of others.

10

A DANGEROUS PATH

Tony Gregory has been an independent TD for one of Dublin's poorest constituencies since 1982. Dublin Central encompasses much of the north inner city, an area which has suffered major crime and drug problems, as well as high rates of unemployment and general social deprivation.

The operations of the various criminal drugs gangs have impacted heavily on the lives of his constituents and Gregory has therefore taken a detailed interest in crime, including its reporting and portrayal in the media. He has regular contact with most of the crime correspondents in the national media and, when Veronica Guerin began her crime reporting in the *Sunday Independent*, he paid attention.

In August 1994, Veronica began her series of articles on the murder of Martin Cahill, in which she claimed that the killing had been carried out by a north inner-city criminal gang, and not solely by the provisional IRA as had previously been believed.

On September 11, the *Sunday Independent* published the third part of her investigation into Cahill's death, again with an exclusive tag beside it and her photo byline. The headline read: 'I'm Threatened In Underworld Battle for City.' The reporter had progressed from detached, non-involved observer, to someone who was talking directly to criminals, learning their rules, and now also very definitely a player in their game. She was now apparently under threat. She had been working for the *Sunday Independent* for just over eight months.

The story, written in the classic breathless style of the newspaper, also featured another stylistic hallmark – the deep identification of the story with the reporter and the dramatising of her own role within it. Elsewhere in the paper, her colleagues were writing first-person accounts of doomed love affairs. Veronica was detailing, in similar style, her own disturbing involvement with people who were, at the very least, violent; at worst, psychopathic.

Veronica wrote:

A vicious battle for control of the Dublin underworld between criminal gangs and the IRA is brewing in the aftermath of the murder of The General, Martin Cahill, according to senior Gardaí.

'Dublin city is currently like a tinderbox just waiting to explode,' said a highly placed security source.

Since Cahill's murder three weeks ago, detectives have received information that other people are at risk, including me.

Gardaí from the serious crime squad in Harcourt Square were informed this week that I was under threat from a named north inner-city criminal. They said they were treating the threat seriously and were keeping my home under observation.

The threat arose from an article published in this newspaper three weeks ago, identifying the north inner-city criminal's involvement in Martin Cahill's murder and reporting that the IRA and the criminal had a prearranged deal to kill Cahill.

Gardaí are aware that since then six other Dublin criminals have been interviewed by the IRA. Some of the criminals made themselves available for interview, others were forcibly taken for questioning . . . the criminals were asked approximately thirty questions, including whether or not they had any contact with me.

In reporting on the alleged threat to her life, Veronica and her employers were breaking new ground. Crime reporters had been threatened before; one of Veronica's older colleagues told me of similar threats to his own life down the years. He received Gardaí protection and took his own security precautions. Wisely, he did not broadcast the fact that he was a target.

There was further analysis inside the main news section of the paper, but in the magazine element of the paper, the Living and Leisure section, Veronica had written once again about Cahill's private life, in an article headlined 'The General's Two Women'.

The headline itself was misleading because Veronica had discovered the existence of a third sister, with whom she claimed Cahill had also had a sexual relationship. Again, most readers of the paper would not have found this revelation of any great significance, but it did have great importance in the real and deadly drama that Veronica was playing out with her informant.

According to a Gardaí source – one of Veronica's main sources for certain of her crime stories – Cahill's alleged relationship with the third sister was known to few people. Veronica had already reported that she was getting personal information about Cahill from an associate. Now, in revealing this highly confidential detail of Cahill's private life, she had all but identified her source. And the Cahill family were making their own deductions very fast.

The usual justification for reporting this salacious and irrelevant detail of a criminal's private life was trotted out once again. This was an attempt, wrote Veronica, 'to understand the criminal mind'.

She was, she wrote, fascinated; how could a man of Cahill's criminal abilities hold such a tenuous emotional arrangement together? 'For many years there had been rumours that Martin Cahill had been the lover of two women, his wife and her sister. Then the rumour expanded. Cahill had taken a third sister as his lover. But the tale always proved slippery, elusive, destined to remain forever filed as myth, rather than fact.'

Veronica then went on to discuss her investigations into the three sisters, and the love they held for Dublin's most wanted criminal. A story, she wrote, 'all the more remarkable for its lack of rancour'.

'Martin Cahill was a vicious, sometimes sadistic man . . . But the cruel gangster who saw humanity in pressing a steam iron into a man's face was also the loving partner of three sisters.' It is highly unlikely that Veronica wrote this story in this way. It has 'house style' stamped all over it, and was more than likely pieced together by a sub-editor or editor. Veronica probably supplied nothing more than the bare facts; the purple prose was entirely uncharacteristic of her work.

But Tony Gregory was unconcerned by the prose style of Veronica's reports surrounding the killing of Cahill. What did concern him was her linking of The Monk to his murder. The north inner-city criminal was known to Gregory and the articles worried him.

Tony Gregory was already well familiar with Veronica's work. His long-standing fight against crime led him to pay close attention to every relevant story in the Irish media. But this was the first evidence, for him, of the risks she was taking.

'Cahill was a south-side criminal, so I would have only known of him from what I had read. What drew my attention to that was the very clear implication in the articles she wrote that a north inner-city gang was involved. Anyone with any knowledge of the criminal world would have recognised the gang and recognised the main person involved.'

Gregory reminded me that initially the Irish National Liberation Army had stated that it was responsible for the killing. It is possible that they had already been planning to kill Cahill, and communications might have broken down to the extent that they believed their own activists were responsible.

But their cache was stolen when the provisional IRA not only claimed responsibility but also provided exhaustive and authentic details of the killing, down to the calibre of the gun and the licence number of the motorbike used for the getaway.

The culprit, who wore no mask, had also been seen by a

number of eyewitnesses. All of which struck Gregory as deeply confusing when he read Veronica's accounts.

> What surprised me more than anything . . . was that these were front-page articles in the *Sunday Independent*, they were labelled as exclusives . . . given a certain status.
>
> When you're reading something that's presented in that way, you like to feel that you're reading something reasonably close to the truth. This didn't seem to be like that. It seemed to be a set-up more than anything else. The 'exclusive' was totally at variance with the known facts.

One of Veronica's articles spelled out the damage that could be caused. It ended with a short paragraph stating that the Gardaí were concerned that gang warfare could break out on the streets of Dublin. It seemed to Gregory that such articles were not only warning of the dangers of a gang war. They were – perhaps innocently and inadvertently – constructed in such a way as to make that war inevitable. They had identified, to those in the criminal fraternity, a figure who they claimed was Cahill's killer. Even though the public information on the subject indicated that it was the provisional IRA. 'The nature of crime in Dublin is that it doesn't take an exclusive front-page article to produce a retaliation . . . something far less than that could bring about a retaliation. The view would have been; there's no smoke without fire. People would have wondered: what's the connection? Did they help out the Provos?'

At the time, Gregory felt certain there was something missing. So he did what he regularly does when trying to build an objective picture of any criminal activity in which he is interested. He rang the Gardaí.

A senior Garda in the serious crime squad told him that he was correct. There was no connection between the north inner-city gang and the General's murder; that what Veronica had written was, to quote the officer who spoke to Gregory, 'reckless' and 'written without regard to the consequences'. Gregory took note.

The Garda told Gregory that Veronica Guerin had called him incessantly, wanting to speak about various crimes. And in his opinion, she was not to be trusted. The Garda said that he was unable to have a conversation with her. Even if it was made clear that what he told her was confidential and to be used only as background information, he felt there was a strong danger of her quoting him out of context, or stating what he wanted kept secret.

As Gregory knew, the Gardaí take a dim view of journalists whose reporting of crime is irresponsible. And hence it was no surprise to hear critical words spoken about Veronica Guerin. 'But to me he had confirmed that what she had written was wrong and . . . it put me off having any dealings with her after that. A number of times when she contacted me, I just didn't return her calls. Two things concerned me at that time. One was the articles and the other was the view of this Garda, who seemed to be reasonable and was just giving me advice.'

Gregory decided to write to the *Sunday Independent* with a view to having his views published in the Letters to the Editor section of the paper. He sent the following letter on September 14 1994:

Dear Editor,
    Veronica Guerin's article on the shooting of Martin Cahill 11th September '94 concludes that the 'Gardaí are fearful that the current climate will result in more murders in the city'.

    The Gardaí's concerns are understandable, most particularly following Ms Guerin's two 'exclusive' articles, in which she claims a north inner-city criminal gang killed Cahill. From details in her stories, the gang is readily identifiable.

    Could anything be more calculated to contribute to that 'climate of fear'?

    In the emotionally charged aftermath of the General's killing, to publish such allegations without any evidence must be irresponsible.

    All the more so, given that her exclusive revelations are

by all accounts without foundation and most likely simply untrue.

Had her story resulted from thorough investigative journalism which had uncovered facts useful to the Gardaí investigation, then it might have some justification.

But to target and set up identifiable individuals for Cahill's murder without a shred of evidence, is not what one might expect from a major national newspaper.

Ms Guerin avoids the fact that all of that 'leading north inner-city criminals group' are known to the Gardaí, their photos are on file, and, as we know, there were numerous eyewitnesses who could identify Cahill's killer.

Did Ms Guerin (who appears to have extensive Gardaí contacts) or her editor bother to check her provocative story with any of the appropriate Gardaí at, or above, the rank of superintendent? I doubt it.

The best that can be said about Ms Guerin's articles is that they were recklessly written and published without any regard for the possible consequences.

It only takes one gunman to believe that there is no smoke without fire, to start a gang war.

The question has to be asked, what motivated those who fed the story to her?

Perhaps Ms Guerin and her editor might check this out and publish their findings.

Gregory wanted to inject an element of balance into the rash claims being made by Veronica; to point out that the articles were not only at variance with the facts, but that the consequences could be severe.

The *Sunday Independent* refused to publish the letter. Gregory rang the paper and spoke to one of the senior editors.

'He said that some of the wording and the terms used were a problem, that Veronica mightn't like them. So I said, tell me what the words are and I'll change them. So he gave me five or six sentences, and I rephrased them and faxed the letter back and waited in the belief that it would be published.'

The *Sunday Independent* still refused to publish the letter.

Even though Gregory made it clear that he had spoken to the Gardaí, that his facts were checkable, and that, while his conversation had been confidential, he was using exactly the words the Garda had used in his description of Veronica's articles – recklessly written and without regard to the consequences.

I felt that this might encourage the *Sunday Independent* to publish the letter, but it didn't have any effect. In the course of my conversation . . . I said that I would have thought his concern should be to present the truth . . . and not exclusive articles that are fabricated and bear no relation whatever to the truth. And his reaction was – what the hell, aren't they just criminals?

So that seemed to be the editorial policy; that what Veronica was writing didn't matter; she was writing about the dregs of society, she was writing about criminals and consequently as long as it was interesting and people liked to read it, they didn't really care whether it was the truth.

Over the years, various journalists have asked Gregory if he ever felt threatened, and how he dealt with that fear. Gregory always answered that he never felt at particular risk, because he had always been meticulous about every statement he made.

I double-checked everything. My view was that, as long as you kept to the truth, there was some sort of unwritten code.

You were entitled to say that heroin is destroying our kids and that so-and-so is living off it and buying it, because that was something that the dogs in the street knew, the Gardaí knew and that was upsetting, but it was OK.

That may have been a very naïve view of mine, but I felt that if I wanted to get at one of these people and made a statement that, say, someone I knew only to deal in hash was actually a heroin supplier . . . in order to draw the cops more on him, I would have felt I was asking for it.

Gregory's view of Veronica at that time was of someone new to the job, hungry for stories, over-enthusiastic and prepared to be led astray. Perhaps she shared the attitude that, since her subjects were criminals, it was permissible to say anything about them.

Gregory still does not know whether the north inner-city gang in question had any involvement with the murder of The General. He thinks that it is highly unlikely. And none of them have been killed in retribution, which suggests that the wider criminal fraternity do not believe that they were responsible.

Whatever the truth behind the murder, Veronica's articles went, in Gregory's view, well beyond her remit as a journalist.

One of the articles said categorically that the leader of this gang killed The General. She wrote about a climate that was being created; but the thing is, the articles *were* the climate; they were creating the climate.

I didn't give a damn about this guy one way or the other. I just felt that the thing was so blatant it required a response. Presenting the story as it was presented was going to achieve what she was saying – a bloodbath.

If the *Indo* had said, fine, you have a point there, then maybe as her career as a crime correspondent developed, it might have been different. It was as if they were saying to her at the time, we don't really care what you write; it's good sexy stuff and as long as people read it, that's OK, off you go.

The *Sunday Independent*'s refusal to print his letter was, to Gregory, a reckless decision: dangerous for the constituency he represented, and even more dangerous for Veronica.

They were encouraging her down a very dangerous road without considering the type of people she was dealing with. I mean the individual that we're talking about, by repute, whether it's correct or not, had been involved in several murders for far less cause than what was being written about in those articles. And that didn't seem a cause of concern, it didn't even seem to dawn on them that they were dealing with very, very dangerous people.

It is, he maintains, clearly the responsibility of the media to expose criminals, but it can be done only on the basis of a factual account of their actions. 'If you say blatant things about people whom you know to be unstable and, by all accounts, extremely dangerous . . . God knows where it could lead.'

Gregory believes that it was Veronica's earliest pieces for the *Sunday Independent* that put her at the greatest risk. Towards the time of her killing, he says, she was using consistently accurate information, writing far more balanced pieces. But her editors are still at fault. 'If she had been checked, or if the editorial policy had reacted a bit more responsibly, maybe that might have helped further down the road . . . I don't know if she'd still be alive but she was giving out a certain image, a certain perception of herself to these people.'

If Gregory, and the Garda to whom he had spoken in confidence, felt that her claims about the killing of The General were inaccurate and irresponsible, how would the criminal fraternity itself have reacted to them? 'The ones that she was getting closer and closer to as her career developed? I would assume they regarded her as someone who couldn't be trusted and whom you couldn't deal with.'

It is not clear whether Veronica herself knew the implications of what she had written. The excitable, schlock-horror tone of her reports suggested that she did not. She was not necessarily responsible for their written style, but she was the sole source of the information they relied upon. They would not have presented any claims that she did not want to be made.

A Gardaí source told me that Veronica's actions, in effect, put a 'death sentence' on the man she implied to be responsible for the killing of The General. It is improbable that she cannot have perceived the implications of that for herself.

For the next few weeks, late September and early October 1994, Veronica moved away from the direct gangland stories, concentrating instead on the Gillane murder case.

It was evident from her reports that doorstepping was standard practice, arriving unannounced usually at houses and offices where clearly she was not welcome, and refusing to go away until her target agreed to talk. She would return again and again, dropping letters by or simply banging on the door and demanding to talk to whomever was inside. Sometimes she would sit for hours outside a house, occasionally ringing her husband on her mobile for cigarettes and food.

There was nothing necessarily untoward in all this. Doorstepping often yields superb stories. But Veronica used the device indiscriminately; there was no one she thought too dangerous to doorstep.

Throughout her time in journalism, she doorstepped politicians, the child of a politician, crime victims, armed robbers, murderers, suspected murderers, drug dealers, bereaved spouses, an alleged child abuser, and a variety of other people in the news at particular times. She showed no discrimination – an approach to a known or suspected psychopath was carried out as nonchalantly as an approach to a harmless politician.

Another disturbing feature of the way she worked was her tendency to take her young son with her on some of her stories. Since Veronica worked alone and secretively, there is no way of knowing how often Cathal went with her. In the *Image* interview carried out in 1994 and referred to above, Veronica had said that she took her son on assignments with her. He was then four years old.

But she did tell at least one colleague of how she had brought Cathal with her when she doorstepped a Dublin man suspected of killing his wife. That man was subsequently charged with the murder.

When the man opened the door, Veronica started to chat but the man's attention was drawn to a child's camera that Cathal was playing with. Fearing that this was a set-up, that Veronica was using her child to get a photograph, he became angry. She told her colleague that it took her some time to calm him down.

By the end of 1994, Veronica was reportedly finding out

that criminals have their own way of dealing with people who threaten their equilibrium.

Just before 10 p.m. on October 7 1994, shots were fired through the living-room window of her north County Dublin home. According to reports at the time, Veronica and Graham had been putting Cathal to bed. No one was in the room at the time.

The *Sunday Independent* reported soberly on the shooting that weekend. Reporter Don Lavery wrote the story. Beside Lavery's report was a photograph of Veronica's house – a strange move for the employers of a journalist who now appeared to be under threat and whose private life and movements were surely to be kept under wraps. Veronica was quoted in the report as saying, 'The Gardaí are satisfied that it was meant to show what the men could do.'

Jimmy Guerin had a more complex reaction to the incident. 'I didn't really realise the extent of her crime work until the shots went through her window. She was working for the *Sunday Independent*. I didn't think it was a good paper and I still don't, so I didn't buy it.

'I never really realised who she was writing about until the shots went through her window. I thought it was silly the way she concentrated on Martin Cahill and I think, after the shots, she became obsessed with these people in a dangerous way.'

Jimmy Guerin was worried, even before shots were fired through her window, that his sister might be going too far. He describes her as being 'far too intrusive of people's very private lives'. 'Does it really matter if Martin Cahill was sleeping with two sisters?' he said to me. 'I don't think it's good journalism to sit outside someone's house for three days or to deliver fifteen letters to ask them to talk to you . . . I think that's silly.'

Jimmy Guerin believes it was bad practice on the part of the *Sunday Independent* to allow Veronica single-handedly to act in such a manner. Had she not been so conspicuous, he feels, she would not have been so aggressively warned off by the criminal community. Her newspaper should not have allowed her to have the monopoly on crime reporting, or even on the business of doorstepping.

'Maybe Veronica would have told them to get stuffed if her editors had done that, but it's too much to allow one person to delve into the criminal underworld that obsessively.'

The incident of shots through her window created a brief stir, says Jimmy Guerin, but people rapidly became complacent. The action was treated as a response to her revelations about Martin Cahill's private life. Nobody saw it as a direct attack on Veronica's life. People – Veronica included – saw it as a warning, nothing more.

Jimmy Guerin assumed, as did others, that the warning would have had the desired effect; that Veronica and her employers had become more careful. As we shall see, this was far from true.

He describes Veronica's own attitude to the incident as typically pragmatic. 'When we [the siblings] would get on to Veronica and tell her to realise what Mam was going through, she'd go down and charm the pants off my mother and then Mam would say to me, "Don't be annoying Veronica, I just spoke to her," which is just pure family politics.'

The Sunday after the shooting, Veronica had an interesting story on the front page. She reported that Martin Cahill had been involved in stealing a file about the controversial death of Fr Niall Molloy in the mid-1980s, from the office of the Director of Public Prosecutions. It is reasonable to assume that the source for the story was the 'associate', who had earlier given her details of Cahill's private life. Veronica reports that an 'associate' of Cahill had allegedly returned the file to the DPP.

The story of Molloy's death was recounted not in the news pages, but in the Living and Leisure or 'lifestyle' section of the paper. It began: 'A nine-foot bloodstain . . . pointed the way to the body . . . '

Veronica's reconstruction of the 1980s' murder fed the popular appetite for such stories. It coincided with a TV series, *Thou Shalt Not Kill*, which featured dramatic reconstructions of controversial Irish murders from the past.

The reporter did not appear to be too disturbed about the incident at her home. Some of her friends and colleagues were not even told about it until a few days after it had happened. But for the next two months, November and December 1994, Veronica concentrated on non-gangland stories. She continued her coverage of the Gillane case and also reported on the murder of Dublin woman Grace Livingstone in her home in Malahide (see page 42).

Gardaí involved in the Gillane case were very obviously feeding the reporter good information. Ennis detectives had spoken to a woman whose lover had allegedly confessed to killing Philomena Gillane. Veronica interviewed the woman at length in an article accompanied by the woman's photograph.

The woman's claims were reported without comment from Veronica; perhaps the Gardaí had deliberately fed the information in order to provoke a reaction from a suspect, or suspects. In any event, this was more proof of the reporter's ability to get further inside a story than any of her colleagues.

Veronica then began a series of reports on clerical paedophilia, reporting, in a front-page exclusive, that the Attorney General's office had not acted for seven months in processing the Fr Brendan Smyth extradition case. Smyth was wanted on child sexual abuse charges in Northern Ireland. The controversy over the delay would later lead to the fall of the Reynolds-led government in November 1994. By any criteria, this was a very good story.

In December 1994, Veronica had another Living and Leisure spread. Her editors had decided that James Livingstone's account of how he had found the dead body of his wife Grace on his return from work some months previously was appropriate 'lifestyle' fodder.

It was a good interview. Livingstone acknowledged that he was a suspect in the case. He spoke of how that felt and gave his own theories about his wife's murder. Veronica had spent a long time gaining Livingstone's trust, using her old technique of simply turning up on his doorstep again and again.

In January 1995, Veronica was back on the gangland crime

beat, this time with a profile of the man she called The Coach. The article was headlined 'The Coach Who's Taken Them All for a Multi-Million Ride'.

In terms of Veronica's crime reporting and the build-up to her murder, this was a key article.

The Coach was Veronica's key contact in the crime world. She gave him the nickname. His real name was John Traynor; he was the former 'associate' of Martin Cahill to whom Veronica had already alluded in several articles as the source for some of her information about Cahill, including the more salacious details of his private life.

At the time of her death, Traynor was a 49-year-old Dublin businessman, a self-confessed criminal with a string of convictions for housebreaking, fraud, firearms possession and handling stolen goods. He was also the owner of a garage in Rathmines, Dublin and the Naas Auto Shop in County Kildare.

He sustained his first criminal conviction when he was nine years old, for housebreaking. Later he received seven or eight convictions for housebreaking and assault. On his last conviction in 1977, he had received a five-year sentence for possession of a firearm with intent to endanger life. He also served two-and-a-half years of a seven-year sentence in the United Kingdom for receiving stolen bonds.

John Traynor was Veronica Guerin's single biggest source in the criminal underworld. He left Ireland shortly after she died. He went to Spain – which has no extradition treaty with Ireland – and has not yet returned to Dublin. He is reported to be running a bar on the tourist strip near Malaga. In October 1997, he was briefly arrested in Amsterdam along with another suspect in the murder investigation, Brian Meehan. Meehan was held in custody to await extradition. Traynor was freed.

Traynor was also a friend and associate of John Gilligan, the self-confessed 'chief suspect' in Veronica's murder and the man who, she alleged, had beaten her up shortly before she died, and threatened to rape and kill her young son. In an interview with journalist Liz Allen in the *Sunday Tribune* five days after Veronica's murder, Gilligan said that he knew he was the chief suspect in the murder investigation, and he denied the charge. At the time of writing, Gilligan is in H.M. Belmarsh Prison on the outskirts of London, fighting extradition to Ireland on charges relating to the Guerin murder; money laundering, drug trafficking and possession of firearms.

Veronica had known Traynor for some time before she wrote her profile of The Coach. None of the people interviewed for this book knew how she had met him. He may have been her source for her inside story on the stolen Beit paintings. A Gardaí source may have talked about him. Ironically, one of Veronica's uncles was the landlord of Traynor's Rathmines premises.

She and Traynor would meet in different places, sometimes for lunch or dinner. A favourite haunt was the Golden Pond Chinese restaurant in the suburb of Rathmines. One of Veronica's friends was alarmed at her apparent closeness to the criminal. She told the friend on one occasion that Traynor had a season ticket for Leeds United matches at Elland Road. She offered to secure it for him. The friend declined.

Three months after she died, the *Sunday Independent* published a lengthy article about Veronica and her relationship with Traynor. The article acknowledged that Traynor was – as the *Sunday Independent* put it – Veronica's 'Deep Throat'. It also included a partial transcript of a conversation that Veronica had conducted with Traynor shortly before she died, and which she had surreptitiously recorded.

There is evidence in the transcript that Traynor did give sensitive information about named criminals and alleged crimes to Veronica, though it is impossible to judge from his words the degree of exaggeration or simple invention in his stories.

One passage in the *Sunday Independent*'s article concerned the murder of a builder called Paddy Shanahan.

Traynor: I'd say I'm one of the only people in Dublin who knows who did 90 per cent of the hits in the last year – who do you think killed Paddy Shanahan?

Guerin: Well – I don't believe it was [she names a suspect].
Traynor: [Names another man] did it from prison – your
man what was trying to stroke [repeats first name].

The article quoted journalistic and Gardaí sources confirm-
ing that Traynor was a major source of information for
Veronica and that he was, at least initially, flattered by her
interest and might even have been attracted to the journalist.

A friend of Veronica's was quoted as saying that she had
taken comfort from a number of conversations she had conducted with Traynor after she had been assaulted by
Traynor's associate John Gilligan shortly before she died. The
implication was that Traynor had talked to Gilligan, and that
Gilligan had expressed remorse for what he had done. In
other words, Traynor was allegedly suggesting that Gilligan's
threats to her family could now be discounted.

But the article also suggested that Veronica's attitude to
Traynor had changed just before she died, that she had
discovered things about him that disgusted her. In the course
of my researching this book, one of Veronica's closest
Gardaí sources told me that she had told him that Traynor
too had assaulted her very shortly before she died. According to the Gardaí, the assault had left no marks on her body
and none of her friends appear to have heard about it. But if
it is true that he did attack her, that would explain the
change in her disposition in the weeks and days leading up
to her death.

But back in January 1995, the criminal and the reporter
were clearly getting on very well. Veronica's article was
deeply flattering – Traynor depicted as a master criminal,
adept at making the Gardaí seem like fools.

The opening of the article was the stuff of crime fiction
novels: 'His mind's eye holds a vivid picture, an image of a
man in a Swiss hotel room, running greedy fingers through a
fortune. He has good reason to remember the scene, for the
man in the picture is himself, and the cash in his hands is
almost one million pounds.'

She quotes him as saying, 'I'm the best in the country at

fraud, and if I didn't live such an extravagant lifestyle, I'd be a millionaire.'

She also describes some of his more colourful scams. He claims that he stole and cashed cheques made out to the Collector General by changing the name to Collette Gerhardt. She details his lifestyle and personal possessions. He denies as 'bullshit and begrudgery' the allegation that he is involved in drugs.

She ends the article: 'The Coach's patch is Dublin's south side, where it is generally considered he has assumed a greater role and increased authority since the death of The General. The younger criminals, once following Cahill's tune, now regard The Coach as their boss. Still, the danger threatens.'

The danger certainly did threaten for Traynor after this article, not for its contents *per se* but because it revealed him as Veronica's source – the Cahill associate who had already given her a great deal of lurid information about his life.

The earlier references to the 'associate' were vague enough to allow him the benefit of the doubt; now there could be no doubt that John Traynor was talking frequently and at length to Veronica Guerin. By dubbing him 'Coach', the play on his surname acted as proof enough.

One week later, on January 29, Veronica wrote another key article. This was based on a brief interview she had held with the man she would identify in later articles as The Monk. It is not clear if the man was known as The Monk at this stage, if the nickname was an invention by journalists, or if Veronica had made a decision, based on caution, not to use it.

The Dublin criminal – a 'very good armed robber' according to Gardaí sources – was the man she had earlier identified as the killer of Martin Cahill – the charge that one of Veronica's Gardaí sources described as a 'death sentence'.

The inside article, headlined 'Criminal Mastermind with Ice-Cold Eyes', is preceded by a front-page report claiming that the criminal is the main suspect for the recent raid on the Brinks Allied security firm premises in Dublin. She details the planning behind the raid and reports that the suspect was prevented from leaving the country at the last minute.

The inside report also details Veronica's earlier attempts to talk to The Monk. She said that when he had eventually agreed to an interview near her home some days earlier, he had failed to turn up. One hour later, she said, the Brinks Allied raid took place. She writes: 'He was a most unlikely-looking criminal mastermind. Almost nondescript, a smiling man looking younger than his 31 years, but with a penetrating, disconcerting stare. We first met last July.'

She reports that when she first called to his door to ask about his financial affairs, he told her to 'clear off from here. Get away from my door.' She says that when she eventually got him to talk, he was 'good company'. I have learnt that this interview took place in a coffee shop.

But later on, Veronica would meet the man again, in the kitchen of her home, for a prearranged interview in connection with a story about him carried in the *Sunday World*. A reporter colleague of Veronica's told me that The Monk simply turned up at the entrance to her home, telephoned her from his mobile and was immediately invited in.

But another source told me this was not the case, that the interview was set up by an intermediary at Veronica's request. The source told me that The Monk had agreed because he needed to convince the reporter that he was not involved in Cahill's death. He needed to make her believe it because he needed her to print it, or at least to spread the word around.

But back in January 1995, The Monk and Veronica had other agendas. She wrote: 'He denied any links with the IRA, but confirmed he'd been interviewed by the organisation after the Widow Scallan's pub bombing.[1] He claimed he was being set up by someone, that Gardaí and other criminals were "trying to mix it" with him.'

The interview with The Monk was published on January 29 1995. The following day at 6.45 p.m., according to Veronica, a man wearing a motorcycle helmet came to her front door and when she opened it he shot her in the right thigh. This attack took place just over three months after shots had been

1 A Loyalist paramilitary attack on a pub in Dublin.

fired through a window in her home.

The shooting was a major story. Veronica was by now a very high-profile journalist – her famous interview with Bishop Eamonn Casey had first catapulted her into the limelight; the earlier shooting at her home had heightened public awareness of her work.

In hospital, Veronica was operated on to remove the bullet. The injury was not serious and she remained in hospital for less than a week. She later told friends that she was receiving counselling to come to terms with it, yet some who visited her in hospital spoke of how untraumatised she appeared to be.

The incident generated great publicity for both Veronica and the *Sunday Independent*. The *Irish Independent* published a photograph of Veronica in her hospital bed speaking to Tony O'Reilly on the telephone.

The following Sunday, six days after the shooting, the *Sunday Independent*, not unnaturally, gave major prominence to the story. On the front page' was a picture of Veronica, her husband Graham and their son Cathal, smiling happily into the camera. The headline over the story read: 'I believed I was about to die. It was terrifying.'

The front-page story carried a declaration by Veronica that she would not be intimidated, that she would continue her crime reporting.

I have said already, and I will say it again now, that I have no intention of stopping my work. I shall continue as an investigative reporter, the job I believe I do best. My employers have offered me alternatives . . . any area I wish to write about seems to be open to me . . . but somehow I cannot see myself reporting from the fashion catwalks or preparing a gardening column . . . I do not consider myself a brave woman . . . In deciding to continue, I am merely doing the same as any of my journalistic colleagues . . . I am simply doing my job. I am letting the public know exactly how this society operates.

Veronica was making this statement within days of being

shot, within days of an operation on her leg, within days of being under heavy medication, which she herself acknowledged had had a disorientating effect on her mind.

This was hardly the time to make decisions about her future, hardly the time to make dogmatic statements of her intent to continue her highly dangerous work and to allow them to be printed on the front page of the country's biggest-selling newspaper.

Veronica's first-person account was on an inside page, beside an editorial which praised the paper's journalist. It read: 'The extraordinary courage, calmness and tenacity of Ms Guerin, her determination to pursue her investigations to the fullest, are to be admired.'

Veronica described how she had been talking to her friend Lise Hand on the phone, had heard a loud knocking, had ended her chat with Lise and went to open the door.

As she lifted the latch, the door was forcefully pushed open. Veronica said that she fell back against a hallway door and then she saw a gun pointed directly at her head.

She wrote: 'My eyes were just fixed on it. It was long, grey, steely, shiny, and was pointing directly at me.'

Instinctively, she wrote, she covered her head with her hands, and curled into a foetal position on the floor.

'My head was still turning backwards, looking at the gun which I now distinctly felt against my leg. This all happened in a matter of seconds and I was screaming – or rather roaring – as all this was going on. My roars came from the pit of my stomach and I can remember them coupled with the noise of the shot. It wasn't a bang, it was more like a roll of thunder.'

The man then fled, she wrote. Veronica, bleeding from the wound in her leg, dragged herself up the hallway to a phone. She rang the local Gardaí station in Coolock and help arrived within minutes. She was taken to hospital and operated on. Neither Graham nor Cathal were in the house at the time.

The focus shifted to discussing who had been responsible. Circumstantial evidence pointed to The Monk. After all, the attack had taken place within 24 hours of the publication of

Veronica's story about the criminal. The *Sunday Independent* already appeared to have judged him guilty. An editorial stated:

> Last week, the *Sunday Independent* investigative reporter, Veronica Guerin, was vindicating a principle: the public's right to know more about the challenge to law and order from Dublin's new criminal underworld.
>
> Her article focused on the background of the man suspected as the mastermind behind the recent Brinks Allied raid who, she claimed, benefited from the tax amnesty. Yet the public was assured by Government Ministers at the time of the Bill's controversial passage through the Dáil that this could never happen.
>
> Last Monday, within hours of publication of the story, Ms Guerin was shot and wounded on the doorstep of her own home.
>
> The attack was meant to intimidate and silence an investigative journalist and, by implication, anyone else who wished to examine the murky background of a new criminal élite which has carried out a series of major crimes . . .

But another story then began to circulate about the alleged motivation behind the shooting, although the origin of this theory is unknown.

One fact was true. The Monk was not responsible for Veronica's shooting, but, so the theory went, Veronica's interview with and story about him had provided good cover for the individual who was later widely suspected of being responsible for the attack – John Traynor.

Traynor, it was explained, was a 'mouth'; he talked liberally to Veronica about his own crimes and about his criminal associates. It is virtually certain that Traynor was the source of much of her information about Martin Cahill, notably the more salacious details of his private life. The revelation about Cahill's involvement with not one, but two, of his wife's sisters was critical; only people who were very close indeed to

Cahill had known about it. Traynor would have been in that small circle.

When Veronica wrote the flattering profile of Traynor, using the nickname The Coach, it was crystal clear that not only was Traynor her source, but that he was giving her a lot of information, information that other criminals wanted kept private. This supposedly put pressure on Traynor to act. There was widespread suspicion that he arranged both of the early attacks on Veronica: the bullets through her window and the bullet through her leg.

In interviews after her death, Traynor admitted that he had allowed people to believe that he was responsible (see Chapter 12). He denied that he was, but he allowed the story to circulate, because he said it gave him 'street cred'. More importantly, it also got any angry criminal associates off his back.

It was also reported after her death that Traynor had either told Veronica directly that he had arranged to have her shot, or that she had eventually figured it out for herself, although the source of these reports was unclear.

But Gardaí at the highest level dispute this theory of Traynor's involvement. Very senior sources have told me that, while they do not know who did carry out this shooting, they do not believe that Traynor set out to injure or kill her at that stage.

Furthermore, the ballistics report on the shooting uncovered certain facts about the shooting that have continued to puzzle those who investigated it. According to informed sources, the bullet had been doctored. It was a 'recycled' bullet, i.e. it had been used before. The charge in the bullet was also extremely low. It lodged in Veronica's upper thigh, lacking the velocity to go through the bone and exit. This would tend to scotch the theory that the attack was intended to kill her. The bullet was also damaged. It looked as if it had ricocheted off something, perhaps coins in a jacket pocket. Yet Veronica's clothing was intact.

This sort of detail, which began to leak out from the Gardaí, married to the fact that no one was ever charged with the shooting, led to a spate of rumours in media, legal and other circles that Veronica had either shot herself or arranged to have herself shot, in order to promote her image as a crime reporter *extraordinaire*.

Senior Gardaí, even those most deeply loyal to Veronica's memory, admit that the theory was given some consideration. One such source told me that he had ruled it out, because anyone who did such a thing would have had to be insane; the risks involved were huge. Even a bullet with a very low charge could still rip through an artery and kill. Yet many of his colleagues continue to harbour deep suspicions about Veronica Guerin's own involvement.

It is remarkable that, even after Veronica's death, Gardaí close to her were still prepared to entertain the 'self-inflicted' theory in relation to the earlier shooting. It is remarkable not just in itself, but also because, at the very least, it suggests that senior Gardaí and those in the lower ranks thought that they were dealing with an unstable personality. But they continued to deal with her, in spite of those suspicions.

As for the theory that Traynor shot Veronica because he was himself in danger from those loyal to Cahill, there is a deep irony. If the theory is true, then Veronica Guerin was not shot in January 1995 because she exposed the criminal doings of evil men; she was shot because she had allowed herself to write about the sexual behaviour of a criminal. She was shot because she wrote that Martin Cahill watched porn movies and had an illicit affair. She was shot for allowing her own standards to match those of the *Sunday Independent* by writing the sort of titillating, intrusive articles so beloved of her employers. Writing which, as much evidence suggests, was far from Veronica's style.

In the immediate aftermath of the shooting, Veronica told colleagues that she suspected that The Monk had organised the attack. She went to confront him in a highly bizarre manner, and one which succeeded in drawing even more attention to herself.

The Gardaí had given Veronica and Graham an escort to their home from the hospital on the day she was discharged. She was still on crutches. One hour after arriving home, she told Graham to get the car. She said she wanted to leave letters at a number of addresses in Dublin. According to a later account by Graham, they went to an address in the north inner city, to Rathmines and one or two other places. At each address, Veronica either left a letter or talked to people who came to the door.

The Rathmines stop was possibly Traynor's business premises. The inner-city stop-off was at the former home of The Monk. Veronica was immediately recognisable to neighbours and others who saw her hobble to the front door, knock, and then leave a letter. Some were shocked, others amused at the sight of the injured journalist just out of hospital, daring to confront one of the neighbourhood's most celebrated criminals.

Was this the act of someone operating along rational lines? Veronica was, as usual, being publicly brave and defiant, but this was a woman who had reportedly come within inches of death just days earlier.

Instead of allowing herself time to rest and heal and come to terms with the enormity of the event, she was throwing herself right back into the fray, applauded and lauded by her employers, who stated that her decision to continue with her investigations made her 'a credit to her profession'.

One cannot help but wonder if, had she backed off, she would still have been such a credit.

Meanwhile, her family was becoming increasingly concerned for her safety. Jimmy Guerin told me that he was particularly worried. He recalls going straight to the Beaumont Hospital when he heard about the shooting from the Gardaí at Coolock and berating her about the risks she was taking, in strong language.

'Everybody was in there kissing her and telling her she was wonderful and I told Veronica that she was a fucking eejit and that she'd want to cop herself on and let this be the end of it, and to cut the shite . . . '

When he came out of her room, he made his feelings known to two reporters – but his stand was undermined when Graham Turley came out and made declarations along the lines of 'We won't be deterred' and 'Veronica's the brains of the operation'.

As well as noting that his sister seemed 'shell-shocked', Jimmy Guerin reports that, after Veronica's editor Aengus Fanning went in to visit her, she told Jimmy that it was only the second time she had met him since she had joined the paper. That night Fanning gave a press conference.

Jimmy Guerin is adamant that Veronica played no part in her own shooting.

I mean we joked at home that they'd found Graham's shoes (in the back garden) and all that type of thing. But we were joking and we knew we were joking, but there were journalists who actually begrudged the fact that she was shot . . . what a fucking sick society.

I heard what people were saying from other journalists. C.J. Haughey told me that he'd heard it, and P.J. Mara had heard it and Seán Haughey.[2]

I think some people half believed it, people who'd known her for years, and it got right up my fucking nose, right up it.

It was at this point, Jimmy Guerin insists, that he lost his respect for the world in which his sister worked. 'I thought journalists were the shittiest shower of people I had ever met in my whole life.'

He describes the effect on Bernadette Guerin, their mother, as terrible. 'I had to tell her . . . she was at a bridge game. So I walk in on the game and I was in there with four hundred old ones, and as soon as she saw me she thought something was wrong. I had told my mother when my father died, and when her sister died; I always seem to get landed with the bloody bad news. So I brought her out and I told her Veronica was shot in the leg and she had a terrible reaction.'

2 P.J. Mara was Charles Haughey's government press secretary in the late 1980s and until 1992. He now works as a PR consultant, but is still involved with Fianna Fáil and acts as an occasional adviser to the party.

Jimmy's annoyance was growing. When he took his mother in to see Veronica, they had been forced to use the back entrance of the hospital because of the crowds. There were also people at his mother's home. 'I was really annoyed. Someone rang the house from one of the papers and I expressed annoyance.'

But then he received word from Graham Turley, via Jimmy's brother Martin, that he should not speak to the press.

Jimmy felt an increasing anger over Veronica's risk-taking, and about the paper which he saw as being behind it. He claims he was not alone. 'I'm being held out as the only one who has this problem with the fucking *Independent*, but at the time she was shot dead, I wasn't.'

When Jimmy heard that Veronica had been round to the house of the person she suspected of shooting her, his anger doubled. 'I flipped when I heard that this was so fucking stupid.' He suspects that it was a publicity stunt performed on behalf of her newspaper. 'Veronica is now like a fucking megastar. "Oh, she's been shot, let's get photos like the Pope kissing the ground when he got off the plane." People were losing sight of the reality, the importance, the seriousness of it.'

Jimmy Guerin not for the first, or the last, time hit the nail on the head when he made this outburst. Veronica, quite evidently, did not see herself as playing a game. But nor, in the aftermath of this traumatic event, did she seem to see herself in the traditional role of a journalist, or, more importantly, as a vulnerable human being whose identity and whereabouts were known to various dangerous people. In visiting The Monk at his home, she had adopted a public, almost superhuman profile, and the consequences of this became not merely serious or dangerous. They became fatal.

11
THE CLOSING MOVES

Veronica was put under Gardaí protection immediately. Within weeks, characteristically, she rebelled against it. She told senior Gardaí that she could not operate under surveillance. How on earth could she meet with criminals if her every move was being followed and monitored by the police? She begged the Gardaí to have the protection removed. One senior Garda argued forcefully against it. Finally, he gave in, telling her to make a formal request in writing to have the protection removed. This she did.

Within weeks of her being shot, Veronica was back at work. Throughout March and April, she moved away from gangland stories, concentrating instead on a controversy involving Bishop Brendan Comiskey in the Diocese of Ferns in County Wexford. She also wrote about alleged Gardaí corruption, the Gillane case once again, and the disappearance of a young American woman, Annie McCarrick.

But by late April, she was back to gangland crime. She had little choice, given her front-page refusal to get out, read by an estimated one million readers of the *Sunday Independent*. Her April story was about the laundering of proceeds of the Brinks Allied robbery. She claimed to have been threatened while researching the article. Her description of the build-up to the threat provided further insight into Veronica's relentless pursuit of her prey.

Alluding to three people alleged to have been involved in the escapade she wrote:

One man associated with Mr Big, involved in the clothing industry, said he had had no property interests and he was struggling to make a living.

When I put it to him that there were records in the registry of deeds, he said, 'Somebody must have bought them in my name.' He denied he knew Mr Big. He said the airport picture must have been someone else. 'You probably think I am some big drug dealer but I assure you I am not . . .'

Last weekend I travelled to Kildare and Kilkenny to meet [another man]. His mother told me that she did not know anything about her son. She didn't know when to expect him.

Veronica then drove to that man's Kilkenny home, purchased the year before for £200,000, and met his father, who gave her an address in north Dublin. It was apparent from the article that Veronica did not tell the father who she was. When she got to the Dublin house, she was told that no one lived there. So she drove back to Kilkenny, again taking enormous risks.

'The father drove in behind me. "Aren't you the newspaper reporter?" he asked. He had a stick or bar in his hand and told me that I had thirty seconds to get out of his yard before he smashed every window in my car.'

In May she had another front-page exclusive. She wrote that the gang responsible for two recent kidnap attempts was believed to have extorted money from a Kildare businessman and a Dublin barrister by holding their families hostage.

In the report, Veronica provided several clues about the identity of some of the people involved, although none would have been identifiable to the casual reader.

She wrote that a 'leading criminal operating on Dublin's south side is believed to have access to machine guns'. She quoted 'a source close to the criminal' as telling her that one of the machine guns had been rented out.

Veronica's knowledge of gangland was expanding. The Gardaí were giving her a lot of information; Traynor and possibly other criminals were also helping out. It is not clear at what point Veronica became aware of John Gilligan and his alleged criminal activities. Prior to being assaulted by him, she had never mentioned him in an article.

Like Traynor, Gilligan left the country after Veronica's murder. But at this time he was living in County Meath, where he and his wife, Geraldine, ran Jessbrook, a major equestrian centre.

Gilligan was certainly well known to the Gardaí, though not so well known to the media. He first gained notoriety through his involvement with the Factory Gang, a group of criminals who specialised in stealing goods from warehouses. This gang stole from premises located in south city industrial estates in Dublin. He had served time in prison.

On his release from prison in the early 1990s, Gilligan very quickly became immensely wealthy. Gardaí believe that part of this wealth came from drug dealing, but the vast bulk came from cigarette and tobacco smuggling – a highly profitable activity when run on a major scale.

Gardaí believe that Veronica was either tipped off about Gilligan by one of their colleagues or that it was Traynor himself who told her about him. Gilligan was a much bigger fish than Traynor; it was inevitable that he would whet her interest.

In late May 1995, Veronica interviewed an unnamed woman who had been subjected to harassment from drug dealers after her teenage daughter had become involved with a young drug dealer and user. It was an intriguing human-interest story, but the most interesting part was the last paragraph, where Veronica once again showed the degree to which she herself was becoming immersed in the world of crime.

She wrote: 'From the description Anna gave me, I have been able to identify her visitors. They are all well-known drug dealers in the south-east Dublin area. Their names and details of Anna's story have been passed to the Gardaí with her permission.'

What Veronica claimed to have done was a correct and

civic act. If she could do something to protect this woman from further harassment, then she had a moral obligation to do so. But why broadcast the fact that she had done it? Why draw the attention of obviously dangerous men on to herself? Was it not enough to alert the Gardaí to what was going on and let them deal with it? And even if she did want to draw public attention to what she had done, did the *Sunday Independent* have to print it?

One week later Veronica was back on the front page again, with a story guaranteed to win her approval from the Gardaí. The story concerned a controversial search in Cork for the bodies of three missing men. The Gardaí had located the site where the bodies were believed to have been buried but, much to the embarrassment of the Gardaí, one of the bodies was surreptitiously moved while the site was supposedly under surveillance.

Veronica provided an apologia for the embarrassed ones. It was an overtime ban and not incompetence that had caused the problem, she declared. Veronica occasionally wrote stories in defence of the Gardaí when they fell under attack for supposed incompetence. One senior Garda said that this was noted and welcomed by all Gardaí.

'That sort of thing helped us a lot,' said the Garda, 'and we would have felt that Veronica was someone we could trust, someone who should be helped.'

The mutual support resulted in at least one bizarre incident. Veronica confronted a man in Cork who had caused consternation among local Gardaí after making very damaging allegations about one member of the force. She went to his home, turned her tape on, and. according to one close colleague, 'berated' the individual until he broke down and admitted telling lies. She then passed the tape on to the Gardaí, suggesting they might like to use this evidence against him.

By this stage Veronica was no longer just a journalist. She was a reporter, detective and private investigator rolled into one. She now saw her role as nailing the criminals, finding the evidence to convict them – not in the courts, but in the pages of the *Sunday Independent*.

She admitted as much herself in an address she had given at a drugs conference, which was published after her death. In a revealing statement, she wrote:

> My newspaper hoped that we could identify these people by name and show the public that their money and wealth was from drugs. I worked many, many hours trying to get the evidence which would enable us to name those guys, but unfortunately it just wasn't available.
>
> So we began writing about their lifestyles and activities and gave them nicknames. Some of the names had been given years earlier by the police, others we made up ourselves. The Irish public have become very familiar with our drug barons, but know them as The Monk, The Coach, The Gambler, The Viper, The General, The Penguin and others.
>
> We are not glamorising these guys by so naming them. What we are doing of value is that we are highlighting inadequacies in our system.

Not all her crime correspondents supported Veronica's analysis of her (and, by extension, their) role. But then few of her colleagues operated in a similar manner. One person who came close was Johnny Mooney, who worked for a period with the *Sunday Business Post*, and now works for the *Ireland on Sunday* newspaper. After her death, he reflected upon what she had been doing.

What set Veronica apart from other crime reporters, Mooney told me, and ultimately placed her in a special category of danger, was that she published the details of her job, and not just the information, if any, that she procured. The story, in effect, was the manner in which she went about getting the story.

'There've been journalists,' Mooney said, 'who have talked their way into the confidence of INLA people, but they never publicised it. They just used it as a source of information. They didn't say, "We went out and we tracked down and spoke to the OC of the INLA." But Veronica would write, for example, "I have spoken to a man called The Monk, or The

Coach," and that's what people would remember; not what they were saying, but the fact that she was meeting them.'

The practice of using nicknames neatly avoided libel problems, but it exacerbated the drama that Veronica's stories were creating.

'I have never heard any of the criminals that I've dealt with refer to, say, The Coach, or The Monk or The Penguin. If you talk to a criminal, he doesn't say, "The Coach did such-and-such." He'll say, "John Traynor did such-and-such." '

In Mooney's view, Veronica's high public profile created a huge problem in terms of her personal safety.

If you're involved in that level of investigation, finding out how criminals are running businesses and criminal activities, you cannot have a public profile.

As far as I'm concerned, if people wanted to call me Joe Doe, I'd be quite happy. It's impossible otherwise; you can't have a picture byline, you shouldn't be driving big or distinctive cars, as she was. Of course, if someone wants to kill you, they'll find you, but in Veronica's case, her profile was far too high to be going around banging on doors.

According to Mooney, Veronica applied tactics – the doorstepping, for instance – that should never have been used in the sphere of crime reporting.

Crime reporting is different because people can kill you. It's a cross between police work, journalism and intelligence-gathering. You really operate more as an intelligence operative than anything else – and what defines that is secrecy.

If you're high profile . . . everyone knows what you look like from television and your newspaper picture, then if you walk up to a door . . . anybody passing by or looking will see you knocking on the door and wonder why a journalist is talking to this person and pass the information on.

But newspapers like the *Sunday Independent* do not want

anonymous journalists on their staff. Rather they want people who will promote their product and who are seen as authorities in the field upon which they report.

By now Veronica had amassed a great deal of Gardaí contacts, both in Dublin and throughout the country. They included ordinary Gardaí on the beat, senior detectives and the most senior officers in the force based at Gardaí headquarters in Phoenix Park. She had an enviable list of telephone numbers, including the direct lines, home and mobile numbers of senior Gardaí.

When a woman came forward to admit that she was the mother of a dead baby abandoned in dramatic circumstances twenty-two years earlier, Veronica marched to the woman's mother's door demanding to know what had happened. She got nowhere, but was able to detail the brief encounter in a bigger story on the incident.

June 1995 was a very busy month for Veronica. On June 4 she detailed the life and times of a group of young dealers, in a piece entitled 'Yuppie Drug Dealing: A Life of Flash and Cash'. She reported that she had visited one of the dealers in his Dublin home.

On June 18 she secured another exclusive by doorstepping her subjects. They were relatives of the murdered Galway woman, Philomena Gillane. Gillane's brother, Paddy Gordon told Veronica about an incident at a fair some days earlier, when he and his brother had allegedly been attacked by an unnamed individual.

The fact that Veronica's visit was not entirely welcomed by the family was gently alluded to by the journalist towards the end of the article. She wrote that a woman, who identified herself as the late Mrs Gillane's sister, had approached Veronica after she had spoken to other members of her family, and asked her 'politely' to leave and not to come back.

None of the stories Veronica wrote that month or the next directly related to Dublin's gangland. They mainly followed the events of the time with an emphasis on human interest.

On July 23 she wrote a curious story about the death of a Wexford man, Michael Murray, a report which came out of the blue and which raised more questions than it answered.

Veronica provided very few facts. Michael Murray had been a happily married man, a former member of a musical group called 'The Emeralds'. He was a devout Catholic, had good business skills and became the controller of funds for the Diocese of Ferns.

At some point in 1990, 'something happened' which led to the break-up of Murray's marriage, his descent into alcoholism and vagrancy. He died, alone, of a heart attack in a flat over a shop in Wexford's main street.

All Veronica could say about the 'something' that happened is that it led to 'his catastrophic disenchantment with the Church'. Friends of Murray whom she contacted, she said, knew that 'his fall related to a particular crisis relating to the Church, but the rest remains mere speculation'.

What Veronica did not report were the numerous attempts she had made to interview Michael Murray's family. At one stage the family grew so distressed that they made efforts through a journalist they knew in the Independent Group to have her called off.

Throughout July and August, Veronica was still off the gangland beat – at least in terms of her published work. She reported on various current stories and had a lot of inside information on an ongoing row over representation within the Gardaí.

But in August, in the Living and Leisure section of the *Sunday Independent*, she was back with more tittle-tattle about the domestic fallout following Martin Cahill's death one year earlier. Traynor had apparently been talking again.

She claimed that Cahill's widow and the two other women with whom he had allegedly had a relationship were down on their luck and had approached friends for money. She quoted one criminal associate of Cahill as saying that he was giving Cahill's widow money 'when he could' out of a debt of gratitude to his former colleague. The associate added that he and his other associates now considered Cahill's family to be 'an unwarranted drain' on their resources.

Then came another bombshell. On September 17, across

the top of the *Sunday Independent*, front page, was a story by reporter Liam Collins detailing a serious physical assault by John Gilligan on Veronica Guerin some days earlier.

Collins wrote: 'A Gardaí investigation is underway into allegations that a Co. Kildare-based businessman assaulted *Sunday Independent* journalist Veronica Guerin after she approached him while researching a story. The man, John Gilligan, who has a prison record, is alleged to have beaten up Ms Guerin and left her with bruises, a black eye and torn clothing after the incident last Thursday.'

Gilligan had also allegedly threatened Veronica in the following manner. He said that if she wrote about him, he would 'fucking kill you, your husband, your fucking son, your family, everyone belonging to you. Even your neighbours.'

Veronica's recent journalism had suggested that she had moved away from her investigation of Dublin's gangland. The assault by Gilligan showed that, even if she had not published anything on that subject recently, she was more involved than ever. For the last number of months she had been seeking an interview with Gilligan, her appetite apparently whetted by the stories she had heard about him from her source and Gilligan associate, John Traynor.

John Joseph Gilligan, known as The Warehouseman or Factory John, was 44 years old and a career criminal. He received his first conviction at the age of 15 on a larceny charge. It was followed by a string of convictions, from receiving stolen goods to assault and battery. It was well known to Gardaí that Gilligan had a violent streak.

By 1995, Gilligan had managed, mysteriously, to create a £4 million equestrian centre, Jessbrook, in Mucklion, near Enfield, Co. Meath. The centre and his home stood on 300 acres.

Through Traynor and other contacts, Veronica had discovered that Gilligan was a significant drug dealer. She was determined to interview him, but he had already declined repeated requests.

On September 14, she drove out to his home and parked outside the heavily guarded equestrian centre. From there, she rang at least one acquaintance on her mobile – a Garda, who warned her of Gilligan's reputation for violence and urged her to drive away.

According to later media reports, Veronica then managed to get through a series of electronic gates – possibly because those monitoring her movements mistook her for someone else – and went right up to the Gilligan home. Confronted by a startled John Gilligan, Veronica began to ask him about the source of his income, but was almost instantly struck on her face and upper body by her reluctant interviewee. After the assault, deeply distressed and physically hurt, Veronica drove off, initially in the wrong direction.

In an interview in the *Sunday Business Post*, published after Gilligan had fled the country, he told reporter Johnny Mooney: 'Guerin was a pain. She must have approached me about ten times for an interview. I kept on telling her to go away but she kept it up. That's why I lost my head when she came to the house. She even had other criminals coming to me, saying she was OK. I told them I'd bend a bar over her head if she came near me. I wouldn't have talked to journalists, not for a million pounds.'

Gilligan denied the assault but did admit to threatening her and to threatening to 'kidnap and ride' her then six-year-old son. He told Mooney:

I knew she didn't fear for herself, so I used a tactic which we use against screws[1] who cause us problems. If a screw's house got turned over, he would get sympathy from his neighbours. They would say, 'Look at that poor prison officer, he's only doing a job keeping criminals locked up.'

So, somebody came up with the idea that you worked the next-door neighbour over, so nobody talked to the screw or his family in case they were next. Instead they blamed the attacks on the screws. It was only a tactic I used to frighten her off, that's all.

1 Prison officers.

Veronica was not frightened off, but the attack had a deeply traumatic effect on her. As she drove, sobbing, away from Gilligan's house, she called a number of people on her mobile, including Graham and several Gardaí. She was distraught. Never before had any of those she contacted, and later met seen her in such a state. Her husband later said that it was the first time she had ever broken down in front of him. She spent the next two days in bed, in pain, fearing that her spine may have been damaged.

It was the alleged intimacy of the assault that so distressed her. According to Veronica, Gilligan had touched her, ripped her clothing, grossly invaded her person through the assault. The earlier shooting had been a curiously detached incident.

But still she was not scared off. Even the appalling threat to her son was not enough to deter her, was not enough to deter the *Sunday Independent* from publishing her work. The day after the assault, Gilligan had rung her and threatened her again. Veronica had by now decided to press charges against him.

Given the assault, given the viciousness of the threats, the decision by the *Sunday Independent* to splash all the above details across its front page was curious and, arguably, inappropriate. It was, of course, a very 'sexy' story: their star reporter allegedly roughed up by a vicious criminal as she bravely went about her work. This could not but be attractive to a newspaper that was now reaching its highest-ever sales figure and which had won priceless publicity from the earlier attacks on Veronica. The front-page story also carried a picture of the security gates at Jessbrook. By this stage, Gilligan was getting very angry indeed.

A few days after the *Sunday Independent* had published Gilligan's threats to Veronica's son, Jimmy Guerin arrived home to find his wife, Lou Ann, in tears. She said that she was upset by the assault, deeply upset at the threats to Cathal and to Veronica's wider family, but more than anything, she was upset at the fact that, despite those threats, Veronica was still determined to carry on.

For the next few weeks, Jimmy and his wife kept their three

young sons close by them, fearing for their safety. At this stage, Jimmy took legal advice, trying to find a way to stop the *Sunday Independent* from publishing his sister's work. He was told that he had no case; that nothing could be done about hypothetical future articles.

Besides, Veronica had not been assaulted because of something she had written. She was attacked as she went about her work in her usual fashion. Her style was, had always been, to push and push for interviews with an intensity that bordered on harassment. She knocked on doors and sent letters and waited in gardens, on paths and on roadsides for weeks on end, until her subject was forced to cave in, or, in this case, was provoked into taking direct physical action against her. If Veronica did not intend to stop doing this, even after a known criminal had threatened to rape and kidnap her son and had brutally assaulted her, there was little that Jimmy Guerin could do.

Jimmy knew that the beating by Gilligan had shaken his sister far more than the shooting incident. He found out about the physical assault only from the *Sunday Independent* account, some time after it had happened, and he knew that it had been deliberately kept from him. 'Don't forget that I was like a fucking raging bull at this stage. I thought that the *Independent* were shites. The beating by Gilligan shook her purely because he ripped her clothes . . . the personal intrusion of dragging her clothes away . . . the humiliation of it.'

He still cannot believe that her employers took no action, other than publicising the beating in lurid detail. 'They saw it as another fucking story. He beats her up and then they get a solicitor on to him and they get another story out of that when she presses charges. It wasn't – let's pull her back; it wasn't – let's take another look at all this. To me, that is so unbelievably, fucking wrong.'

After having learnt from his solicitor that he could take no action to prevent the *Sunday Independent* from publishing future stories, Jimmy spoke to Veronica. 'She went from telling me to piss off and not to be hysterical and not to be stupid, to saying that she was going to watch what she was doing. But then she went ahead and carried on . . . '

He believes that, by this point, a worrying change had taken place. 'Veronica was under more pressure – between the time she was shot in the leg and the time she was murdered. She'd lost the bubble, she'd lost the spark. Now it was becoming just a job; she was under pressure to deliver.'

He does not doubt that it was a self-imposed degree of pressure. 'If she didn't feel like doing it, she would have told them to naff off . . . but she was taking too much on.' Whether it was self-imposed or not, Jimmy maintains that she was 'carrying too much responsibility' and being portrayed by her paper as an icon. 'She was shot in the leg and she was still going to fight the cause . . . ' Bolstering her image as a public and conspicuous opponent of dangerous underworld figures was, he says, exactly the opposite of what the *Sunday Independent* should have been doing at the time. 'She was owed guidance, or discipline, or help . . . ' Veronica's biggest fear was peer pressure. That's not meant as disrespectful to Veronica; we all have different things that push our buttons. But Veronica didn't want to be seen to give in.'

She was back at work within days of her assault. Throughout October, she focused on the controversy surrounding the sudden sabbatical taken by the Bishop of Ferns, Brendan Comiskey, following a reported row with the Vatican over comments made by the Bishop about clerical celibacy.

Veronica followed the Bishop to the United States. She believed she had tracked him down to a private clinic in Florida. A picture appeared of Veronica standing in front of the clinic, accompanied by an article saying how she had tracked him down and why she believed he was in this clinic.

It later emerged that Comiskey had never attended the clinic in question. Veronica openly apologised for her mistake to the Bishop at a press conference he held some months later on his return to Ireland. She came in for a lot of criticism, not just for her mistaken report on the clinic, but also for the fact that she had hounded the Bishop in the first place. She stoutly defended her integrity and argued that her pursuit of the Bishop was journalistically valid.

At the time of his departure for the United States, Comiskey had come under scrutiny following rumours of a cover-up in relation to child sexual abuse cases involving members of the clergy in his diocese. He defended his handling of the matter and was never found to have acted improperly. There had been other reports about the Bishop's purchase of an apartment in Dublin, none of which unearthed anything untoward, and the Bishop's holidays to Bangkok in Thailand had also been investigated by the media.

In an interview published after her death – a contribution to a student thesis on investigative journalism – Veronica said something quite revealing about the episode:[2] 'If I am to be really honest about the circumstances of my going to the States, I would have liked to have spent a few months out there persuading him to talk to me – it was an editorial decision and I will stand over it.'

Veronica appears to be suggesting that the decision to run with the instant story, including a photograph of herself standing outside the clinic she only suspected Bishop Comiskey was in, was made by her editors, and not by herself.

A friend of Veronica's told the author that Veronica's hand had been forced in this instance by her editors. He had contacted her on her return to berate her for running the story. He told her it was bad journalism and beneath her. Veronica told him she agreed, but that her editors had pressurised her to go with it, pointing out that it had cost them a lot of money to send her to the United States.

For the remainder of the year, Veronica concentrated on the stories of the day. In October she briefly returned to gangland with a report on how three of the top drug dealers in the country had come into the tax net during the period of the tax amnesty. She quotes one as saying, 'I'm legit and they can't touch me.'

November 1995 was dominated by reports on the so-called 'Tuffy' affair. Pat Tuffy was revealed as the author of a series

2 Interview with Kitty Holland, as reported in *The Irish Times* of June 27 1996.

of anonymous letters to the then Fine Gael minister Michael Lowry, claiming that Lowry was under surveillance by a group of Fianna Fáil-linked businessmen. When Tuffy then claimed that the Minister himself had put him up to writing the letters, it was Veronica who first 'deconstructed' his claims in an interview she conducted with Tuffy. It was good, solid journalism.

For the first three months of 1996, Veronica only briefly strayed into the area of gangland crime. She wrote a wide variety of stories, including the Marilyn Rynn murder investigation;[3] follow-ups on the Bishop Comiskey affair; the aftermath of the IRA bombing of Canary Wharf, which ended the first IRA cease-fire of the peace process; the controversy over a shortfall in Football Association of Ireland ticket sale receipts; and an exposé of traveller-linked crime.

Veronica was ahead of the posse in many of these investigations, again demonstrating her near-unrivalled ability to secure excellent inside information.

But not everyone was enamoured of her investigative zeal. In April 1996, she reported the murder of a female Dutch national, Anne Marie Duffin. She wrote: 'A local man obsessed with murdered Dutch woman Anne Marie Duffin may have killed her in a jealous rape attack over her relationship with another woman . . . she was intimately involved with another woman.'

A reader responded:

I feel I must express my utter disgust and sadness at the lack of sensitivity shown by Veronica Guerin to the family of the late Anne Marie Duffin, RIP, regarding her so-called intimate relationship with another woman . . . I don't know whether this is true, nor is it any of my business, but I can only consider the feelings of her two sons, who must face their friends at school following this 'gutter journalism' . . .

---

3 Marilyn Rynn was a 41-year-old civil servant who was brutally raped and murdered while walking home after an office party. Early in 1998, a local man was convicted of the murder and sentenced to life imprisonment.

I wonder if Veronica has children herself. I will not be reading the *Sunday Independent* again.

Towards the end of March, she was back on her old beat. She interviewed Fr Paddy Ryan, a priest with strong and controversial republican links. He talked to Veronica about his association with criminal elements, including the late Martin Cahill. Very little of substance emerged from the interview, but it was evident that Veronica was not letting go of her old interest in gangland; she was still probing, even if she was not yet prepared to publish the results of her investigations.

Veronica was also reporting on another highly controversial story at the time: the apparent seizure by the Gardaí of a huge cannabis haul at Urlingford on the Dublin to Cork road. The haul had at first been billed as a major coup for the Gardaí – it was, they said, the biggest such seizure in the history of the state. In fact, the Urlingford seizure was the result of a semi-botched Gardaí operation. They had seized the drugs; but not from the large truck at Urlingford. They had set up a type of 'sting', taking the drugs from a ship off the Cork coast, pretending to be the intended recipients.

The intention was to arrest the real recipients when the drugs arrived at their destination, but a breakdown in communications led to that plan being abandoned. In the end, they were forced to stage the Urlingford 'seizure', but many people smelt a rat.

The Gardaí were accused of importing the drugs themselves. The truth was somewhere in between, but the Gardaí were forced into a defensive PR exercise. Veronica was fully briefed on the truth, and helped to get the Gardaí out of the hole they had dug for themselves. In some political and media circles, she drew criticism for swallowing the PR line, for being a 'Gardaí lackey'. But it does appear that everything she wrote was accurate.

At the end of March there was another significant twist in the story of Veronica's pursuit of Dublin's gangland criminals.

In much of her crime reporting, Veronica and the *Sunday*

Independent were competing against their rival, sister newspaper, the *Sunday World*. Paul Williams was that newspaper's crime correspondent and he too had printed his share of exclusive crime stories. He had also written a book on Martin Cahill.

Williams tended to rely more on the Gardaí for his stories than the criminals themselves, but was still able to secure a great deal of information about the drug dealers and others. Nonetheless there was an ongoing battle between Paul Williams and Veronica, and at times it appeared that each was attempting to up the ante.

In late February, the *Sunday World* raised the stake. It printed a large, front-page photograph of a youngish man, his identity barely disguised by a thin stripe of print across his eyes. The headline read 'Public Enemy No.1' in huge type and underneath was a litany of allegations against the man whom the newspaper was now, exclusively, naming as The Monk. This appears to have been the first time that the man's nickname had been used.

Veronica obviously had to go one stage further and better than her rival reporter. Williams had gleaned the bulk of his information from the Gardaí; Veronica talked to the man himself. The interview took place at her own kitchen table.

This marks Veronica's most reckless action to that date. She was interviewing a highly dangerous criminal in her home; the criminal with his own agenda and her wanting nothing more than a good story. In addition, she was now heavily involved with another criminal, John Traynor, whose loose tongue was also likely to land him in trouble with other, even more dangerous, criminal associates. The *Sunday Independent* could see no further than its splash headlines; underneath the surface, lethal elements were at play.

Those around Veronica did not appear to see the danger. In an article given to *In Dublin* magazine in September 1996, Graham Turley made a casual reference to that interview with The Monk. Mostly, he knew little about the people his wife was interviewing.

Until one Friday I came home early, and there was a fella sitting in the kitchen, and Veronica was talking away and having a cup of tea or coffee, and I was introduced to this person, and I said, 'Listen, I don't mean to be rude, but I'm in a bit of a hurry, I've got to do some bits and pieces', and rushed by the person and went upstairs, changed and said goodbye and walked out the door.

And the following Sunday, I was in the Rugby Club in Malahide and somebody said to me, 'I hear Veronica interviewed The Monk.'

So Sunday evening, I came home and I said, 'I never knew you met The Monk,' and she said, 'You met him yourself – that was him in the kitchen last Friday when you came home. And that wasn't the first time he was here.'

The Monk talked. But it was in his interests to do so. He was concerned that the *Sunday World* article had labelled him as a drug dealer. For a man living in an area where scores of young people were dying from heroin and other hard drug abuse, this was an extremely dangerous label to carry. He was not involved in drug dealing, he claimed; he needed to get that message across. Veronica had the profile and her newspaper had the necessary clout to do that.

For the first time, Veronica refers to the man by his nickname. The *Sunday World* front page is reproduced beside the article, a convenient way of getting The Monk's picture in the *Sunday Independent* too.

The tone of the article is openly boastful. 'It is rare,' wrote Veronica, 'for a man described as an underworld leader to grant interviews, and The Monk is careful in his choice of words.'

In the interview, the man denied any involvement in drug dealing and told Veronica how his mother was 'sickened' by the thought that he may have been involved. Veronica acknowledged The Monk's reason for giving the interview and graciously conceded the quid pro quo. She wrote: 'Though The Monk's reputation is as a hardened criminal, his claim to be separate from the narcotics trade appears to hold credence. He is the only well-known criminal not named on the IRA hit list of alleged drug barons and a Garda of commissioner rank told me there was no record of The Monk being connected with drug dealing.'

The Monk also used the opportunity to deny that he had any involvement in Veronica's shooting. She believed him, either because he had been sufficiently persuasive or because she knew by now that Traynor was believed to have been the person behind it.

She wrote: 'It was the Brinks Allied robbery that brought The Monk's name to the public eye. This was followed one week later by an incident in which I was shot as I answered my front door. The Monk was immediately identified by Gardaí and the media as the man responsible for both crimes. He denies both, and although he was responsible for the Brinks Allied raid, I know he was not connected with my own shooting.'

That use of the word 'know' suggests that Veronica had in fact known this before The Monk's denial. Veronica's casual acceptance of herself as a player in this unfolding drama is obvious in this article. She had placed herself centre-stage.

The following week, Veronica wrote a longer piece on the same interview in the 'Analysis' section of the newspaper. Her own role in the story was again highlighted. 'When I learned that he would speak,' she wrote, 'I wondered if I would meet the man or whether I would be presented only with his legend. After several hours of interrogation, during which he chose to answer many, though not all, of my questions, I believe I encountered both.'

Her use of the word 'interrogation' is also curious – reporters ask questions, detectives interrogate. Veronica had clearly begun to see herself in a different light.

In April and May, she wrote a variety of stories: ongoing murder investigations; internal Gardaí rows and a report on how confidential personnel files about Department of Justice staffers were allegedly being leaked.

In May she wrote about the investigation into the murder of Wicklow publican Tom Nevin. Apart from one article on

The Monk's 'empire', she steered away from gangland stories.

But gangland was not steering away from Veronica. She was no longer writing about Traynor, Gilligan or his associates but according to reports after her death, some sort of communication was being maintained between the two named criminals and the reporter. She had pressed assault charges against Gilligan. Traynor was growing increasingly concerned about what she might write next. His fears were justified.

Veronica was discussing with her editors the possibility of naming at least four criminals whom she believed were connected in the drugs trade. Traynor believed that she intended to name him and possibly to link him to Gilligan. Veronica was also believed to be trying to link Gilligan with cocaine trafficking.

Traynor hired lawyers to secure an injunction against publication. Just under two weeks before her death, he applied to the High Court for that injunction.

The atmosphere in the wider criminal underworld and in the reporting of that underworld was heightened throughout early June. Veronica had told friends that she was involved in an intensive investigation of one particular criminal. She also said that one of his associates was warning her to lay off.

Two alleged drug dealers were then named in Leinster House by TD Tony Gregory, the names printed in the next day's newspapers. The *Sunday Independent* made an editorial decision to try to name others. According to one colleague, Veronica was wildly excited. The incident in Leinster House was the very opening she needed.

One of the men named by Tony Gregory was Tommy Mullen, up until now referred to in the media as The Boxer. Gregory's move gave Veronica an excuse to confront him and write about him openly.

In this she was helped by a Gardaí source. The source had been keeping an eye on Mullen for quite some time. The man had a low profile few of his neighbours knew about his alleged activities.

Veronica was not just serving her own purposes in this, but

also those of the Gardaí. A photograph of Mullen, the publication of his address and a photograph of his house would be very helpful for any of the anti-drugs community activists anxious to root out the dealers in their areas.

On June 16, Veronica reported on her attempts to interview Mullen. She said that she had left several messages for him, in her usual fashion, and that he had eventually contacted her to answer her questions. He claimed that all his money had been legitimately earned. But his picture was printed, as was the address of his house.

It was later reported that Mullen's home was raided by the Gardaí the day after this article appeared.[4]

By this stage, it was clear that a number of bodies were benefiting directly from the risks Veronica was taking – her employers, certain criminals and the Gardaí. But if she was being used, it is certain that she would never have seen herself in this light. She was a willing participant in everything she did, or was asked to do.

Around this time, another frightening event occurred. The windows of her car were smashed, an act believed in hindsight to have been an attempt to see if they were bullet-proof. Some Gardaí sources believe that this was not the case; they say that the windows were smashed out of anger at yet another attempt by Veronica to extract certain information from one of her criminal contacts.

On Sunday, June 23 1996, Veronica's final article for the *Sunday Independent* was published. She reported on the life and times of drug dealer Tony Felloni, who had that week been sentenced to twenty years in prison. She interviewed his wife, who talked about her drug-addicted children. It was a superb piece. But its worth becomes overshadowed by the events that took place three days later.

Just before one o'clock on Wednesday June 26, Veronica Guerin stopped her car at traffic lights on the Naas dual carriageway just outside Dublin. She was returning from a court

4 In January 1998, Mullen was sentenced to 18 years in prison in England for drugs trafficking. He was described as one of the biggest heroin dealers in Ireland.

appearance in Naas, where she had been fined a hundred pounds for a speeding offence.

At the lights, she dialled the number of a Garda friend and spoke to his answering machine. She laughed that she'd got away with it; that she hadn't been disqualified or banned from driving. She was still talking when two men in black leather jackets drew up beside her on a large white motorbike.

The pillion passenger alighted, produced a large revolver, went to the driver's window of Veronica's car and pumped five bullets into her chest and upper body.

The Garda whom she had phoned later played her last message on his machine. He heard her laughter, the friendly taunts, the sounds of the bullets, a brief cry from Veronica and then silence. She had died instantly. The rest was an outpouring of grief, a river of flowers outside Leinster House, the adult heartbreak for the small boy left without his mother.

This is how Cathal was told about Veronica's death by his father; Graham recounted this to journalist and family friend Seán O'Rourke on RTE radio shortly after she died. While Graham had gone to identify her body, Cathal had stayed with his grandmother. Graham arrived at the house with the local parish priest, Declan Doyle, another friend of the family. The boy was playing with some Lego when his father came in.

I sat down on the chair and said 'How are things?' and he said 'Grand, Dad.'

He had been kept away from the television and the papers and nobody had said anything to him. So I said, 'Cathal, do you remember the last time Mum was shot? Well it's happened again.' And he said, 'Yeah? Where was she shot this time?' And I said, 'She was shot in the heart.'

And he came over and sat on my knee and he comforted me. And Declan said to him, 'Cathal, can you make a courthouse?'

And Cathal said, 'Yeah.'

And we made the court-house in Naas, and we made two cars and a motorbike, and then he asked, 'Who was on the motorbike?'

And I said, 'Well, there were two men on the motorbike, and they seem to have been wearing black helmets. And they pulled up alongside Mum, and they shot into the car and hit Mum.'

'Where did they hit Mum?'

And I said, 'They hit Mum three times around the heart, and they hit her in the neck.'

'Is Mum coming home?'

And I said, 'No, she's not coming home, but she's going to be here minding us, because remember we talked about this before?'

'Oh, I got it,' he says. 'She's with God now, and she'll be looking down on me and everything I do from now on.'

And it's been like that ever since, that everything we discuss, Mum has always been there and always will be. And we left there, my mother's house, and we went to Stafford's funeral home, and Veronica was there, and we had a chat and a cuddle and a laugh, like we always did, the three of us together. And we talked, and Cathal was saying, 'Mum, you're very cold', and things like this. And then we left.

When Jimmy Guerin first heard the news, he thought it was a joke. He had received a call from a best friend of his at around one o'clock. A mutual friend, who worked in the newsroom of an Irish radio station, had passed on the news that Veronica had been shot.

'It's terrible to admit this, but we used to often ring and say, "I see Veronica was shot", and we'd done this maybe three or four times and the first time it worked and the second time it didn't work. So he rang me and said Veronica was shot, and I said, "Yeah," and he said, "No, no seriously, Veronica was shot." I said, "Look, Seán Paul, fuck off, she wasn't," and so on.'

Jimmy put the phone down, but suddenly had doubts. He rang his wife, and Marie-Therese, his older sister, but they had heard nothing. He turned on the news, and heard nothing.

I went down to the AIB bank in Artane because I needed cash to pay someone and I went in to talk to Philip Foley who's the manager. I'd always go in and go up and have a chat 'cause I know him a long time. And I said, 'Mahon's after ringing and saying Veronica was shot.' And he says, 'What a fucking awful thing to be saying.'

And then I came out of the bank and across the road was a fella who was working with me. And I knew by his face straight away and it just clicked that something was wrong. And he told me that Veronica was shot.

He rang Marie-Therese and other family members, but nobody was in. Still not knowing how serious the shooting had been, he rang his aunt, Colette Cullen. She told him that Veronica was dead.

His wife was distraught with grief, but was at least with people, so Jimmy's first concern was for Bernadette, his mother. At the time, she was attending a neurology clinic at the Beaumont Hospital.

He remembers being very cool and composed as he asked the staff to locate his mother. He was afraid that she might see the news on the television, or in a newspaper, before he could tell her. But she was not at the clinic.

His mother was at the neurologist's practice in Ballsbridge. She had an appointment at one o'clock and then was meeting people for tea in the Berkeley Court Hotel afterwards. The doctor's secretary, upon hearing the news, tried to get Bernadette to go into the sitting room, while she claimed to be looking for her medical records. But Bernadette stayed in the waiting room. It was here that Jimmy Guerin came and told his mother that Veronica was dead.

She was hysterical. I had to put on this act, you know, of . . . strength. So we took her home anyway and the rest of the family came in then and we were gathering our thoughts together . . . and people were calling, which took us up till about half-past three.

We were all in Mam's house. And then Graham [Turley]

came down at about four o'clock with Declan Doyle, the curate. Graham was consoling my mother, sitting there, she couldn't say anything, and all Graham kept saying was, 'I'm so sorry, I'm so sorry' . . . kept saying he should have stopped her.

My mother kept telling him, 'No, don't be stupid.' And people were calling and we were kept busy that way. And Seán O'Rourke called and one of the Assistant Gardaí Commissioners came by. I can't remember his name now but he was probably in his sixties . . . anyway he took my mother's hand and he said, 'I know exactly how you feel.' And she's sitting there like a dummy. Anyway he says, 'I know how you feel because I buried my father three weeks ago.' And my mother said to him, 'What age was he?' . . . 'Eighty-seven.' So all we could do was laugh at that.

Veronica Guerin's body, at this point, was still in her car on the Naas road because the chief state pathologist was at an inquest, and it could not be moved until he had attended the scene of the shooting. Later, Jimmy and Graham went to identify the body at Blanchardstown Hospital. After a long wait, they were shown in at 10 p.m.

'Then Graham went off to tell Cathal with Declan Doyle and I went back to my mother's house, and there was a lot of people calling and everything else. Cathal was asleep, so they decided not to wake him; they'd tell him the following morning. So that was the day. They all reacted in the same way, in apportioning blame . . . they blamed the *Independent* and Graham blamed himself.'

When Willie Kealy, *Sunday Independent* news editor, called the following morning around eleven, he received short shrift from Jimmy.

'I said to him, "You know I attribute – if you want to call it – blame, Willie, well fuck you. You should have known what was happening." '

Jimmy notes that the family, naturally enough, was given over to its private grief. They were oblivious to the reaction of the world outside the door of 26 Bluebell Avenue.

'My mother has her alarm set to the radio. And she normally has it set for half past seven, so that she's up at eight . . . down for mass every morning at nine o'clock. And as she woke up, the first day after Veronica had died, the first voice she heard was Veronica's . . .'

Having decided after that to have no radio or TV on in the house, the entire family was taken aback by the tumult which accompanied Veronica's funeral – a bout of public attention which only exacerbated their grief.

'There was no privacy at all, there was no privacy at the funeral home except for the first night,' Jimmy told me.

The removal of the body, from the funeral home to the church at Dublin airport, was planned for five-thirty. The family intended to leave the house at four forty-five.

Certain government departments had been contacting the family, announcing the intention of various figures to attend the funeral. At about ten o'clock that morning, Jimmy remembers the announcement that Tony O'Reilly himself intended to call on them at home. 'There were actually people coming into the house to see *him*, you know . . . it was fucking unbelievable. I suppose from knowing the Haugheys and from mixing with ministers, that didn't excite me, but people were actually whispering, "Tony O'Reilly's coming round."'

While Bernadette was hoovering in preparation for O'Reilly, a call came from his public relations consultant to announce that O'Reilly would be fifteen minutes late.

'Well, I said, "Mr Milton, this is Jimmy Guerin, Veronica's brother; we're not running behind time and we're leaving at five on the dot."'

The family had specifically asked that no photographers be present, either at the house, or *en route* to the church. The only photographer to break this rule was a man working for O'Reilly, who came to capture his visit. O'Reilly arrived at five to five.

'Gavin[5] was there and he had a yellow polka-dot tie on. I told him it went well with the tan. But I must say he was a

5 Gavin O'Reilly, son of Tony.

terribly nice fella and Tony O'Reilly was a complete gentleman. But my mother hadn't a clue really what was going on
or who was there, and she grabbed O'Reilly on the way out
and told him, "Take those cups into the kitchen." '

On the day of the funeral, Jimmy went early to the church
to plan the seating arrangements for the ceremony later that
day.

There was a fella there walking up and down and he said to
me, 'Can I help you?' I said no, and introduced myself. And
he said, 'Oh, I'm sorry, I didn't realise; I'm from Murrays,[6]
I'm with the Independent Group, these are the seating
arrangements. The family will be here, here and here; colleagues and the media will be here, here and here; the
government ministers here and here, and the Independent
executives here and here.

Now the arrangements were fine, perfect, but I was determined I was going to change something 'cos I wasn't going
to have this little prat in a suit telling me what to do at my
sister's funeral. I said to him, 'You know, you remind me of
someone from Foreign Affairs at an Ard Fheis[7] or at a State
function. This is a funeral and there aren't enough seats
there for my family and my extended family and my in-laws
and my sisters-in-law. So take the working media and your
media colleagues back four or five rows.' So he was running
around, chasing around with seats.

The family's plan was to leave at twenty to ten, to be in the
airport church at nine forty-five, meet President Mary
Robinson, the Archbishop of Dublin and the Taoiseach, and
then proceed to the mass.

But at ten to ten, they still hadn't left the house and Declan
Doyle came out and said to me, 'Look, I've the Archbishop
inside and the President inside the church and they're

6 Murray Consultants – a PR firm.
7 Party Conference.

waiting on your mother, and your mother hasn't left. Will you go in and apologise to the President?'

I felt like saying I'm not going in to apologise to anybody. But he was really in a fluster, so I went in and talked to the two of them and they sympathised and I said thanks. 'My mother was to be here five minutes ago but she isn't up to leaving yet and when she's up to leaving, she'll be along.' Poor Declan was gobsmacked that I wasn't apologising, but the two of them were absolutely lovely about it.

The delay was partially because Mrs Turley, Graham's mother, was waiting outside the Guerin house, unwilling to go in because she felt it would be intruding on private grief. Meanwhile, Bernadette Guerin was in the house and would not leave until Mrs Turley arrived. While Graham's brother, Robert, was trying to persuade his mother to go inside, Martin Guerin was trying to persuade Bernadette to go out.

'That went on for about ten or fifteen minutes until eventually they realised they were waiting on each other. Mary Robinson was lovely; I'll never forget Mary Robinson . . . she came over to Mam and she said to her, "I don't know how you feel and I hope I never do." The first one I had heard being honest with her.'

Jimmy Guerin's words acquire a deeper significance as we go on to consider the events that followed Veronica's funeral. There was an outpouring of grief in which noble statements were thick on the ground, but honesty and straight thinking seemed to be in short supply.

12

THE AFTERMATH

Less than two weeks before Veronica died, John Traynor had applied to the High Court for an injunction to stop the Sunday Independent from publishing an article about him, written by her.

The hearing was finally held on July 1 – five days after Veronica had died. Traynor was by now in Spain, while there was media speculation that he may have been involved in her death. Two affidavits were read out on his behalf. The contents were damning of Veronica and of her work yet, controversially, the Sunday Independent had chosen not to lodge a defence, even though they had been in possession of the affidavits for almost two weeks before the hearing.

Opening the hearing, Traynor's counsel, Adrian Hardiman, pointedly told the court that his side had written to solicitors for the defence, expressing the distaste they felt in urging the application so soon after Veronica's murder and offering an adjournment. The Sunday Independent had declined the offer.

When the issue of the Sunday Independent's silent response to the Traynor affidavit was raised some time later in Phoenix magazine, Sunday Independent news editor Willie Kealy wrote the following letter to the magazine:

Your criticism of the handling of the John Traynor injunction case has already been dealt with in a public statement by the Editor. It was also explained to you personally what happened. The Editor did not see the affidavit of John

Traynor, because he was not personally dealing with the case. I was. We were not devoid of strategy – Veronica was on her way to file a reply to that affidavit when she was gunned down.

In the few days following her death, a period of shock and grief, I received emphatic legal advice against entering the affidavit on behalf of the Editor and myself. I accepted that advice. I now believe that I should not have done so. It allowed a convicted criminal to drag the names of Veronica Guerin and Aengus Fanning through the mud without rebuttal.

Phoenix's charge had been exactly that – Veronica's professionalism was severely criticised by Traynor and the *Sunday Independent* did not on that day say a word in her defence. *Phoenix* had asked 'did nobody in the Sindo [sic] argue against the "unfortunate" legal advice, which had the effect of leaving John Traynor's scurrilous statement unchallenged in court'.

Eamon Dunphy says that the reasons for the failure to make a replying affidavit were quite mundane. It was an error born of shock and confusion in the wake of a colleague's death. He defends the newspaper's record in relation to protecting itself and its contributors, and allows that a 'systems failure' in the management of the newspaper could have contributed to what eventually happened.

Veronica came in to a very successful newspaper and she also worked solo, from home, outside the office. The most striking thing – and it is important to record, because it was the single biggest problem I had . . . was the fact that there were never any editorial meetings. There was never a conference to plan the week; there was never a conference at which you could express a reservation about the direction the paper was taking, or about a particular column that had been in.

Dunphy suggests that there was a 'power vacuum', where

in the normal course of a newspaper's life, individuals would have been able to put a halt to, or at least express their opposition, to trends that they found unacceptable.

Dunphy reports having first had reservations when Veronica was shot in the leg. 'That was a shocking moment and I know from speaking to Aengus that he was shocked.'

Dunphy is adamant that Veronica was never compelled by her newspaper to place herself in danger. 'The *Sunday Independent* bothered about crime because Veronica bothered about it. They bothered about the North because I wrote about it. Aengus did not push Veronica; I know that. And I can prove that he tried to stop her from writing about it.'

Some time after Veronica had been shot and subsequently warned, and had written formally to reject Gardaí protection – Dunphy is not sure whether this was before or after the alleged assault on her – Aengus Fanning called Dunphy. 'He said, "Look, would you come into the office; I want to talk to Veronica and I want you to try to help me explain to her that she should do something different, that this isn't necessary."'

According to Dunphy, Fanning argued with Veronica that the paper was already successful, 'and that a dead journalist or a compromised journalist was no good to him. By "compromised", he meant someone who had to have the Special Branch around them all the time; someone who was afraid because they were receiving threats; someone who was inhibited by danger, such as she was clearly now exposed to. It was no good for her, it was no good for the paper, it wasn't necessary and he didn't want her to do it any more.'

Fanning looked to Dunphy to support him in this.

He turned to me as someone who had not been in danger, but someone who had been doing tough work, and said, 'Eamon will tell you, I don't care if the copy doesn't come for six months', and he really didn't. Because sometimes I had gone off the boil, in the way that you do, especially as a columnist, and I'd tell him I was burnt out and that was OK.

So what he was saying was, look, we value you here; you don't have to up the ante all the time. Aengus understood that pressure, he'd been there himself and that was what made him a good editor, a great editor.

But Veronica's response had been typically wilful. 'She said, "Aengus, if you don't let me do it, I'll go to another newspaper. I want to do it; I haven't finished. I want to do this story and that story," and so on. She said she wanted to out these guys and that was that.'

As they left the office together, Dunphy recalls, Veronica laughed the matter off.

Fanning's attempts were, Dunphy argues, necessarily going to be ineffective against a journalist so obviously driven as Veronica. And the structures were simply not in place to support him. 'This is where the vacuum in the *Sunday Independent* came into play; the absence of any real direction. An editorial conference would have been able to comment on each piece she did and would have given her a collegiate feeling, and would have taken her from that isolated place where she was in the end.'

In spite of the reservations of various colleagues, however, Dunphy told me that Veronica Guerin's death came as an enormous shock.

I was so traumatised by her murder that I have never written – bar one column – for the newspaper since, on anything other than soccer. The traumatisation was absolutely extraordinary, because of the shock, the unbelievability of it.

We were stunned, because it was absolutely incredible that someone could do this and although she had been – for a couple of years – flirting with danger of the most extraordinary kind, going to criminals' houses and so on, I don't think that anyone had a sense that this could happen.

According to Dunphy, the *Sunday Independent*'s chief concern had only ever been the possibility of litigation. 'The only real considerations were libel considerations. It's a huge concern . . . will this article stand up to libel scrutiny? Not will it cost the journalist his or her life, because there was no precedent for that.'

And hence, Dunphy argues, the decision not to respond to Traynor's affidavit was taken in a state of shock and confusion.

I went to the court with Aengus and Anne and Willie and they were in a state of deep shock and I was too. So shocked that when Hardiman offered to withdraw the affidavit, some junior counsel said to us – no, the judge won't allow him to read that out, given the circumstances. And we went to court and it transpired that the judge was obliged to allow the affidavit to be read.

I bawled the junior counsel out about it afterwards, but Aengus was sitting there like a zombie and Willie was sitting there like a zombie. The funeral hadn't even taken place. I can't speak about anyone's feelings of guilt, but I can only speak about my own feelings of deep shock and horror, for her husband, her mother and her child. At that point I didn't detect guilt; I detected horror.

Dunphy notes that the option of refusing to print Veronica's work was never really open. If a piece by her had been pulled, he argues, she would have moved to another paper.

'Subsequently that was used against [Fanning] by people who argued that he should have protected Veronica, but I knew Veronica; she'd have said, "Fuck off, you're not protecting me." She was a spirited individual.'

Dunphy feels that the newspaper profession as a whole may have made the collective error that journalists would not be murdered. There was no precedent for it; and that, given the circumstances of Veronica's murder, there was no way it could have been foreseen. 'She happened to run up against a very unstable criminal who was way out of his league, a cowboy. I think other criminals – organised crime – would have seen how counterproductive it would have been to murder a journalist.'

The account of Traynor's affidavit appeared in the daily national newspapers on July 2 1996. In journalistic circles, much of it was held to be suspect and self-serving. Nevertheless, many of those who had worked with Veronica over the years recognised elements of her tenacious style of reporting. Elements that, when applied to a man with a history such as Traynor's, were likely to have spelled disaster.

According to his sworn affidavit, Traynor was contacted by Veronica roughly a fortnight before the date that he issued his first affidavit – June 14. They met at the Greyhound Bar in Harold's Cross. He had met Veronica on a number of previous occasions relating to articles she wished to write. The following is taken from the account of his affidavit, printed on July 2 1996.

During the meeting, Ms Guerin said she had received from her editor an anonymous Garda report about him from J District, a copy of his previous convictions, and a photograph from a Gardaí file. He was told by her that a paragraph in the report linked him with two named persons believed by Gardaí to be the main heroin dealers in Dublin.

He said the confidential report was never produced to him or offered to him. It was not forwarded to him by Ms Guerin. She said her editor was insisting she publish a story about his connection with these two other people. He said he had never heard of the two people mentioned.

Mr Traynor said he had never been involved in sale, supply or importation of illegal drugs, nor had he ever been questioned by Gardaí or any other police or Customs officers in relation to the sale, supply or importation of illegal narcotics.

In a second affidavit, dated June 18, Mr Traynor said he made application for interim relief on June 14, because on the previous day Ms Guerin had contacted him by phone and informed him a publication highly defamatory of him would be written by her and published on June 16.

For approximately the last twenty months, he had been contacted by Ms Guerin at frequent but irregular intervals. The contacts were followed almost immediately by a meeting in a place of her choosing. He had no choice about attending because, if he demurred or suggested postponement, she informed him it was in his best interest to attend, saying she was contemplating publication about him.

The first meeting was in a coffee shop in Montague Lane, between Camden Street and Harcourt Street, Dublin. She astonished him by telling him details of a social outing – described by her as an 'escapade' – he had had with a friend of his who happened to be a member of the Gardaí. She indicated she was going to publish a story about this and about him.

She engaged him in conversation about the romantic life of Martin Cahill, about whom 'she knew a great deal more than I did'. She discussed various crimes, some of which he had read about and some which appeared fictitious or imaginary. She suggested he was involved in some of these, although the suggestion seemed speculative. He knew nothing whatsoever about the matters she mentioned.

Mr Traynor said that at this first meeting, Ms Guerin suggested he had been instrumental in returning to a Garda a file in connection with a criminal prosecution which had gone missing or been stolen. She asked him to give her a copy of the file.

About a month later, Ms Guerin phoned him again. She said she was doing a story on him, but first wanted to work on the file. He refused to discuss this or any topic and terminated the conversation. She immediately contacted him again, berating him in hysterical terms for his 'non-cooperation' and shouting that she wanted to do a story on him.

On the next day Ms Guerin rang and cajoled him with threats into meeting her in a Leeson Street hotel. At this stage the threats relating to him centred on what she described as the 'escapade' with the Gardaí. She appeared to be threatening him with association of some sort with

147

the 'missing file'. Later the nature of her threats changed and became more specifically related to drugs.

At the hotel meeting Ms Guerin flung down in front of him what she claimed was an original DPP file in relation to a criminal case. She indicated she had the original and did not need a 'fucking copy'. She indicated disappointment with the contents of the file, wondering what was 'so important'.

He said he knew nothing about the case, the subject of the file. He did not think Ms Guerin accepted that. The case related to the circumstances surrounding the death of a priest in the midlands.

Over the next few days, Ms Guerin contacted him on numerous occasions. She told him the Gardaí had given her his phone number. He did not find that credible. He did not know how she came to contact him.

However, Mr Traynor added, the landlord of his premises at Church Avenue, Rathmines, was her uncle and that gentleman's son was a person with whom he was acquainted due to their shared interest in motor racing in Mondello. It was possible she became aware of him through either of those people or in some other way.

Several months later they met in Fans Chinese restaurant on Dame Street. Ms Guerin was extremely friendly and appeared to have lost interest completely in the file about which they had had confrontation. She was in reminiscent mood. She told him about cases she had been involved with, her dealings with police officers who, she said, gave her information about criminals who were police informants.

Mr Traynor said Ms Guerin seemed completely fascinated and obsessed about crime and police work. She talked in terms of 'crims' and 'feds'. She freely mentioned her contacts with both of these groups.

At times, she would appear, or appeared, to become convinced he would tell her details of criminal offences of which in reality he was completely ignorant. She was not suggesting he was guilty of, or in any way involved in, the offences, but merely that he could, if he wished, find out the true facts and communicate them to her.

In recent times Ms Guerin became convinced that the much publicised murder of a Co. Wicklow publican had been a contract killing. She insisted to him with threats that he could find out who had done this and tell her. He knew nothing about this and lacked the means to begin making inquiries about it. He would imagine she was in a far better position to make inquiries, either from police or criminal sources.

She plainly did not accept his denial and again threatened to expose him in some form of story, although at the time it was unclear what sort of story she proposed.

Mr Traynor said apart from occasions such as that described or when she was demanding something from him, and apart from her threats to expose him, the tone of their meetings was almost always friendly.

They sometimes had meals together. Neither of them ever drank alcohol at the meetings. In his case this was due to his belief that she was a serious threat to him even when ostensibly friendly, and at times she appeared to him to be irrational. She told him on occasions the only thing she lived for was a good story, but on other occasions she had to print stories because of extreme pressure from her editor, Mr Aengus Fanning.

She clearly had astonishing sources of information. She was able to tell him matters involving himself such as his social connections with his friend in the Gardaí . . . and a minor dispute he had had about mooring a boat.

Mr Traynor said that in the past two months his contact with Ms Guerin became much more frequent, much more intense and expressly and overtly threatening. He was unable to say precisely what this was.

However, before the start of this phase, an event occurred which seemed to annoy Ms Guerin. He had an altercation with a well-known businessman in Harcourt Street which led to allegations of assault. He was invited to call to Harcourt Square Gardaí station to make a statement about the matter. He did attend, but declined to comment.

Mr Traynor said some time later he was contacted by Ms Guerin, who informed him that there would be no charges and that the allegations had been withdrawn. She said that he 'owed her one'.

Shortly afterwards, Ms Guerin sought his assistance in arranging an interview with Gordon Smith. Mr Smith, whose story was subsequently written by Ms Guerin, was a person who was kidnapped in the Republic by the UVF and Ms Guerin wished to do a story about this.

She invited him [Mr Traynor] to help her arrange this because he was acquainted with Mr Smith's father. She interviewed Mr Smith at the La Touche Club, Earlsfort Terrace, and in her presence and at her request, he paid Mr Smith £100. Ms Guerin was not willing to pay him because she insisted that, on principle, she never paid for stories.

Mr Traynor said a short time later Ms Guerin contacted him once again in her hysterical mode. She alleged to him that she had been arrested and questioned by two Gardaí superintendents on the basis that she was suspected of 'perverting the course of justice' in relation to the matter of the alleged assault. He had no idea whether this was true or not.

Ms Guerin had told him on a previous occasion she had been arrested under Section 30 and alleged on this occasion she had been arrested under Section 4.[1]

On June 3 last, without any intervening contact, Ms Guerin arranged to meet him and told him he was going to be the centre of a major story by her in the *Sunday Independent*. This story, he understood from her, had two quite separate limbs.

The first was that he was involved with – 'connected with/mixed up with' – two men called Mr Murphy and Mr Mullins who were major heroin dealers. The second limb

---

1 Section 30 is the Offences Against the State Act, and Section 4 is the Criminal Justice Act. Under Section 4 the detainment time after an arrest and before pressing charges is shorter than under Section 30.

related to three men from Liverpool or the Liverpool area whom she said had been arrested in Dublin and whom she claimed had been on their way to deliver drugs to him.

Both of these stories were completely untrue. He knew nothing whatsoever about any of the matters mentioned. He was not now nor ever had been directly involved in the purchase or any dealings in drugs or the proceeds of same.

Mr Traynor said he protested in those terms to Ms Guerin. She told him she was surprised, because no one, neither guards nor criminals, had ever alleged he was involved in what she termed as 'heavy drugs'.

She told him her editor had received anonymously, 'in an envelope', a Garda report from J District. She said: 'You're just in a short paragraph thrown in the middle.' She appeared to accept his denial of any involvement because she ended by saying: 'I'll have to look further into it. I don't believe you are involved in it.'

Mr Traynor said he asked her when she would have looked further into it and she said she would have done so the next day.

At the meeting the next day Ms Guerin saw him in the La Touche Club after a phone call in the afternoon. She said: 'I think you are going into the paper.' He asked her why she would do that when she knew it wasn't true. She said: 'My editor is wondering what's going on between you and me when I am not using your name, when I am using others.'

She told him that the two men she had mentioned were going to be named by Deputy Tony Gregory in the Dáil and that he might be so named as well. He continued to protest his innocence and she said: 'I'll have to see.'

He asked her what the story was about the men from Liverpool and she said that she had found out that was not true. She said: 'When they came, they realised the stuff was unsaleable. They were just going to take it back.'

He asked Ms Guerin with great sincerity for the sources of her information. She said her source was two 'crims' and was confidential. This was a long and fraught meeting between Ms Guerin and himself and in the course of it she unequivocally accepted that the story she proposed to print was not true.

She said: 'I know you're not involved in heroin, but I have to print it.' He asked her why. She replied: 'It's your lifestyle, you have a boat worth a quarter of a million pounds and a string of race cars in Mondello.'

Mr Traynor said he had no idea where Ms Guerin got this information. The facts of the matter were that he had a half-share in a motor boat worth £16,000 and he owned three cars used for touring car racing at Mondello. These were respectively valued at £7,000, £3,000 and £1,500. He told her this.

He asked her if she regarded these things as evidence of involvement with drugs and why she didn't investigate everyone in Mondello. She said that the possession of cars by other persons was explicable because 'they have garages'. He pointed out to her that he had two garages.

He told Ms Guerin on this occasion in quite emotional terms about the effect this story would have on him and his family. He said it would destroy his wife and children, force him to move them to different schools, probably destroy his businesses and put him at risk of his life from vigilante types.

Ms Guerin acknowledged all of the consequences. She said: 'I hate my job.' She said she had told her editor that it would put him in danger, but that he was unimpressed. She said in express terms and repeatedly that her editor was making her 'do this'.

In a pattern that was to become very familiar, Ms Guerin was not on this occasion 100 per cent certain that the story would appear and stated she would ring him the next day. The next day – Wednesday June 5 last – she rang him and arranged to meet him at the Greyhound Bar. She told him that she was not doing the story she had previously planned. 'Instead I am going to put you down as a hash dealer. I met two crims who told me you sell hash.'

He said that if she published this story, he would sue her and she could bring such witnesses to court. She said: 'I am not too sure they would go to court.' She then said she knew someone to whom he had admitted selling 'hash'. When pressed, she described the person to whom this admission was allegedly made as being 'the Provisional IRA'.

She claimed that this organisation had made a tape of him making such an admission. When he denied this story to her she again said that she wasn't 100 per cent certain that they would go ahead and she would let him know the next day. He told her that these allegations were completely destructive to him and his family and likely to expose him to a risk of being murdered.

He told her he would go to court to stop the stories.

The following day she rang him and told him: 'We are doing this story.' There was no further conversation. He arranged to meet his solicitor at 9.30 a.m. the following morning, Friday June 7.

On June 7, at about 9.20 a.m., Ms Guerin telephoned him from her mobile telephone as he was driving down Terenure Road to see his solicitor. She said she had discussed the matter with her editor the previous night. She said she had told him that she could not stand up in court, put her hand on her heart and say that Mr Traynor dealt in drugs. Therefore, she said, the paper would not cover the story. He thereupon, perhaps foolishly, cancelled his appointment with his solicitor.

On Monday June 10, Ms Guerin phoned him in the afternoon. She said she was coming back from Limerick, which he took to be a reference to Adare, where two Gardaí had been shot the previous Friday. She said she wanted to meet him the next day.

She rang the next morning and arranged to pick him up at about 1 p.m. at a business premises known as 'Mr Gearbox' on Richmond Road. She picked him up there in her car and drove him to the La Touche. In the course of this meeting she said: 'I think I will have to run the story this week.' She then said: 'I hear how you might be selling "E".' This was a reference to the drug ecstasy. This allegation

153

was completely new and was equally false. He asked her ironically what else would she hear and she said: 'I'm not sure about the "E" but I do know about the hash from these two crims.'

He insisted upon the falsity of this story and begged her, for the reasons already given, not to publish it. She told him she was doing a big story on the Provos, adding: 'I think you are going to have to go in.'

She made an appointment to meet him the following morning at the Mercantile Hotel, Dame Street. She told him they were going to do the story. Their meeting that day was a very long one. She told him she thought they were going to do the story. He begged her with all the power at his command not to do so, pointing out that it would destroy his family and his businesses and perhaps lead directly to his death.

She acknowledged that all of this was true and also expressly and repeatedly acknowledged that the story was false.

Late on Thursday June 13, she telephoned him and told him the story was definitely going in. There was no further conversation.

The defendants proposed to publish a story about him which was false and which, according to Ms Guerin, they knew to be false. There was no prospect that they could prove it to be true, because it was not true and because Ms Guerin's alleged information came from anonymous criminals whom even she doubted would be available to attend court.

On the other hand, this story would be absolutely destructive of him and his family and could well lead to his death. In this connection he referred to an article published by Ms Guerin on June 16 last in which she appeared to acknowledge that to be described as a drug dealer exposed a person to the risk of death.

He knew nothing of the motivation of Independent Newspapers and Mr Fanning except insofar as Ms Guerin had commented on this. He said, however, that Ms Guerin was obsessed with crime, criminals and policemen and was very confident she held a very powerful position.

Several people have noted inconsistencies in some of Traynor's claims. Traynor, for example, alleged that Veronica had told him that the TD Tony Gregory was going to publicly name him as a criminal. That said, Gregory has confirmed to me that when he did name a number of criminals in the Dáil, he did it spontaneously. 'Nobody could have known about it in advance,' he said, 'because I didn't know myself in advance that I was going to do it.'

Traynor's description of Veronica's method is very consistent with what we have seen, repeatedly, throughout her journalistic career: tenacity, persistence, bordering upon aggression. An overriding desire to make the big story, with a significantly smaller degree of attention to the details, ethics, or risks involved.

The affidavit, inconsistencies aside, makes it likely that Veronica's actions brought Traynor to the point of desperation. After her murder, he fled to Spain and has not returned. But in an interview with the *Sunday Business Post*, conducted in September 1996, two months after Veronica's death, Traynor categorically denied any involvement in her killing: 'I'm a straight businessman, I know they think I shot her, to stop her writing a damaging article about me, but it wasn't me.'

When he heard the news of Veronica's death, Traynor claimed, 'I just thought, shit, this is going to be ten times worse than the injunction. That's why I left Ireland. I didn't do it. I never ordered a shooting in my life. You can't go shopping for a hit. I couldn't order that sort of intimidation because I'm not that well connected in the underground. I have a fair idea who was responsible and I know the reason why, but that's my business. 'If I was going to shoot her,' he pointed out, 'I would not have spent three thousand pounds on an injunction before I ordered it.'

In that interview, Traynor conceded that he was under suspicion for the murder, not just because of the articles

Veronica threatened to publish, but because of the earlier shooting of Veronica at her home in 1995.

'I was arrested under Section 30 and questioned on that attack,' he told the *Sunday Business Post*. 'When the guards picked me up I said, "I'll answer everything", which I did, and was released about nine hours later. They know I had nothing to do with it. If they thought I did it they would have kept me in for the full forty-eight hours.'

However, in that interview, Traynor admitted saying to other criminals that he had been responsible. 'I did tell people I ordered it because they started ringing me up, congratulating me for it. I told some people that it wasn't me but before I knew it, everyone believed it was. So, I let them. You could say it improved my street credibility.'

He also denied the suggestion that the earlier shooting was an attempt to win back the favour of the Cahill family, angered by his release of private details to Veronica. 'There is no bitterness between myself and the Cahill family. I did not know about his love life. Martin was not the type of man who would discuss that sort of thing with other men.'

Veronica Guerin trusted John Traynor too much. Socialising with him in the manner that she did – sharing drinks and Chinese meals, discussing football – blinded her to the true nature of her criminal companion. By the time she did become aware of the threat that he and his colleagues posed, it was too late.

Veronica Guerin was not content with reporting crime. She wanted to solve the crimes herself. With her 'informants' and her 'interrogations', she lost herself in a role for which she had neither training nor experience. That, married to the near absence of boundaries in her interaction with the criminal world, led to her death.

To date, as we shall see, the *Sunday Independent* has failed to admit that it played any culpable role in allowing that situation to arise, or that it intends to bring into place structures to prevent a repeat. Its official response, as set out in the following chapter, has been to abrogate its responsibility, and to stress the wilful nature of its employee.

13

NOT OUR PROBLEM

The *Sunday Independent* refused all requests for interviews for this book. They had a good excuse.

On Saturday June 22 1997, I arrived back from a week's holiday. The next day, I picked up a copy of the *Sunday Tribune*, a newspaper part-owned but under the effective control of Tony O'Reilly's Independent Newspapers group.

A headline on the bottom of page one read: 'Guerin's husband angry over Emily O'Reilly book.'

Graham Turley, the husband of murdered crime journalist Veronica Guerin, said last night that he is disgusted at plans to publish a book based around the murder of his late wife just one year after her death.

Dying for the Market,[1] written by Emily O'Reilly, political editor of the *Sunday Business Post* and Radio Ireland presenter, will be published by Vintage in November.

'I am disgusted that this individual has gone ahead with this book without contacting me or various other members of Veronica's family especially in light of the fact that I stated on *The Late Late Show* last December that the family did not want any books or films to be produced on Veronica in such a short time after her death,' said Turley.

Vintage has billed the book as 'an extraordinary story of a bold but reckless young journalist and a forceful exploration of the dubious ethics of modern journalism'.

1 A working title.

157

They also claim that *Dying for the Market* 'exposes the frightening moral bankruptcy of the media'.

Turley said that he doesn't 'know how Emily O'Reilly got her information on Veronica in such a short period of time as she wasn't a close friend of Veronica's.' A number of Guerin's closest friends in journalism have not been contacted either.

Willie Kealy, news editor of the *Sunday Independent*, said that as far as he was aware, none of Guerin's former colleagues at the paper had been contacted by O'Reilly in connection with the book.

It is understood that individuals at the newspaper only became aware of the book last week. None of its executives have been asked for their views on the claims being made about their behaviour.

I learnt later that this report was based on some earlier publicity material for the book, which I had seen, but which I was unaware had been published in a Vintage catalogue some months earlier. It set me back somewhat, since I knew it would now be hard to obtain interviews with *Sunday Independent* executives.

This 'leaked' early publicity material suggested that the editorial line would be hostile to Independent Newspapers. I could hardly disown what the publishers had written, but neither could I go into too much detail about how my thinking about Veronica Guerin had evolved as I had researched the book. I did not want to put my thoughts in writing, because I was concerned that such a letter would end up in the pages of one of the newspaper group's many titles.

I contacted news editor Willie Kealy by phone. He raised the issue of the publicity material, said he would consider my request and contact me in a few days' time. He never did.

I sent registered letters to Aengus Fanning and to the group public relations consultant, Jim Milton. Initially neither man replied. At my request, an intermediary finally got Milton to call me. He too raised the issue of the publicity material and said that I had clearly reached conclusions before I had done my research. I requested a meeting just to discuss the book without prejudice. Milton did not rule it out, but later wrote to me to decline my invitation. He said that he doubted if what he had to say would be treated fairly.

Aengus Fanning and Willie Kealy wrote a joint letter declining to be interviewed. They noted Graham Turley's request for no book at this stage and also the book's early publicity material. They also reminded me of the letter I had written to Fanning and Anne Harris two days after Veronica's death, in which I had praised their role in relation to her journalism. Since they had declined to be interviewed, I was in no position to tell them that after investigating that role, I had changed my mind.

But the *Sunday Independent* has responded to some of the muted criticism of its treatment of Veronica. The only publication that really tackled the issue was *Phoenix* magazine. The BBC documentary, *Dying for the Story*, also raised question marks about the newspaper's behaviour, which were responded to in the programme.

The first broadside came in a profile of Aengus Fanning in *Phoenix* magazine on July 19 1996, just over three weeks after Veronica's death. It was written by Paddy Prendiville, Veronica's close friend, who had for many years attacked the *Sunday Independent* in the pages of the magazine. Its politics were anathema to Prendiville, as was its general tone and style. In recent years, *Phoenix* had begun to refer to the *Independent*'s 'Duckworth School of Journalism' – a reference to Vera Duckworth, the blousy, loudmouth bar manageress in *Coronation Street*.

Curiously, Prendiville had encouraged Veronica to go to the *Sunday Independent* when they began to make overtures. Prendiville remembers: 'She didn't want to leave the *Tribune* but she had to because her relationship with Vincent Browne had deteriorated. She agonised over going to the *Indo* because she hated the *Indo*'s politics, I mean really genuinely loathed them. 'But I told her that she couldn't choose the politics of the paper she worked for. Journalists can't pick and choose their politics like that and, if they can, they're very lucky. I told her in the end that she really had no choice.'

Prendiville and Veronica kept in frequent touch when she moved to the *Sunday Independent*. She talked about her work, but Prendiville told me that he wasn't privy to the sources of her stories. He formed the impression that she had more Gardaí than criminal contacts but he did not know, for example, that she was meeting regularly with John Traynor.

In the last few weeks of her life, Prendiville noticed that Veronica was under increasing strain. 'A couple of times, two or three times in the weeks leading up to her death, she said "I'm tired". The second or third time she said it to me, I thought it was odd, because usually it was me complaining and Veronica was in the best of form. I said, "Why are you so tired? Are you working very hard?" "Jesus," she said, 'I'm working twenty-three-and-a-half hours a day. I'm really under pressure."'[2]

When she died, Paddy Prendiville considered that it was payback time for the *Sunday Independent*. Not only did he consider that the newspaper's journalism was tawdry, he also blamed them in part for his close friend's death.

A great deal of the Fanning profile, published on July 19, was devoted to the general editorial content and ideology of the newspaper. Prendiville raised serious question marks over its credibility and culture and noted the newspaper's consistent promotion of the cult of personality within its pages. 'Promoting the cult of the personality is harmless enough with your average *Sindo* hack, but the danger to serious journalists like Veronica Guerin was obviously underestimated by *Sindo* executives. Not only was Guerin a serious journalist, but she was dealing in the serious world of organised crime.'

Prendiville's profile drew attention to Veronica's indispensability to the *Sunday Independent*. It mentions a qualitative survey and analysis concluded in late 1994, which stated that

2 Another friend of Veronica's told the same story. He noted how tired and drawn she had become towards the end. She spoke about the pressure she was under. It seemed to him that she was no longer enjoying her work, and may even have been considering leaving crime reporting.

the *Sindo* was in many respects seen as 'trivial . . . trashy . . . cheap and sensationalist'. The same survey, according to Prendiville, recommended that much of the tackier material be dropped and that there be more news, investigative and business stories.[3]

Which is of course what Veronica, to an extent, provided for them. 'She had struck the perfect blend, as far as the *Sindo* was concerned, i.e. good, hard news reportage combined with some pretty sensational stories about drug barons, armed robbers and contract killers.'

Prendiville makes it clear that Veronica provided Fanning with a 'lifeline' at a time when he was under massive pressure to make cuts. Various freelancers had been shed and plans to head-hunt superstars, to replace 'departed hacks like Sam Smith and Rory Godson', had been abandoned.

Veronica's impressive work rate and instinct for good news stories was therefore invaluable. When she began to complain to friends about being tired, a complaint they had never heard from her before, it was probable that pressure for more stories from fewer hacks had resulted in a 'perhaps unconscious but definitely increased demand on [Veronica] for stories'.

. Even after she was shot in the leg, Prendiville noted, 'Independent Newspapers' management seemed to be unaware of the very real dangers posed to their journalist.' Only a submission to the NUJ chapel, arguing that her shooting underlined the financial vulnerability of contract journalists – who might be killed or disabled – led to Veronica Guerin being covered by an insurance policy for the first time.

In recent weeks, the demand for more hype in the crime stories had led to a deliberate policy at the *Sindo* of naming various criminals.

The *Sindo*'s insatiable appetite for more crime stories, the heightened publicity surrounding Guerin's personality as

---

3 Prendiville's piece stated that the survey had been commissioned by the *Sunday Independent*, an allegation they have consistently denied. It is believed that the survey may have been carried out by a company in a bid for a commission.

the country's premier crime reporter, and the paper's new tack of outing Dublin criminals combined to render Guerin more vulnerable than ever.'[4]

Prendiville's was one of the first voices to publicly demand to know why Aengus Fanning, her editor, did not rein in his star crime reporter. His was also the first to note that the paper seemed to show no greater concern for her reputation in death. Traynor's affidavit had dragged Veronica's name through the mud. The *Sunday Independent* had not responded. Fanning was unaware of the contents of Traynor's affidavit until he read it in the newspapers on July 2, fourteen days after it had been filed in the court. Six days after Veronica's murder.

'That any such affidavit concerning any of his journalists should remain unread for two weeks by the editor of a national newspaper is difficult to credit in any circumstances. But in the atmosphere of public outrage surrounding his reporter's killing, it is truly remarkable that Fanning should publicly state that he had not even read an affidavit that besmirched the same journalist's reputation, as well as his own.'

Prendiville pointed out that Traynor's solicitor had revealed that he had written to the *Sunday Independent*'s solicitors two days after she was shot, offering an adjournment of the hearing, on the grounds that it was too soon after Veronica's death and would cause distress to her family. The offer was rejected.

Prendiville's piece drew a warm response from the journalistic community. 'The whole episode gave me a huge insight into the monopoly of the *Independent*, into its power and dominance, the fact that people are scared of it,' he told me.

4 There is no evidence that Veronica Guerin had been instructed to publish the names of the criminals. The evidence suggests that she was enthusiastic about the idea, despite the real threat posed by naming those people.

'Everybody, even *Independent* journalists, said I was right in what I wrote, but few of them ever went public.'

Three weeks later, the *Sunday Independent* replied to Prendiville's article. By this stage Jimmy Guerin had written to *The Irish Times* criticising the newspaper's treatment of Veronica and raising questions about its responsibility towards her. The issue could no longer be ignored.

The paper's deputy and news editor Willie Kealy sent the reply. The *Sunday Independent* was still sticking to its original defence of its treatment of the dead journalist. It was all Veronica's fault. Kealy called Prendiville's piece 'a malicious campaign of vilification of the *Sunday Independent* ... a mixture of lies, half-truths, and deliberate misinterpretation of the truth'. Veronica's workload, he stated, was self-imposed. It was even part of his duty to try and manage and restrict that workload for her. Measures were not, Kealy stated, taken to insure Veronica after pressure from the NUJ. 'We were constantly aware, without any prompting, of what was needed in the area and we did all we could within the limits of what Veronica would accept.'

He dismissed talk of reining Veronica in. Anyone who knew Veronica understood that if she was not allowed to carry out her work for the *Sunday Independent* in the manner she considered necessary, she would simply have gone to another newspaper. It was not *Independent* policy to 'out' criminals. It had been Veronica's idea, and one about which she felt passionate. The editor did not see the affidavit of John Traynor because he was not personally dealing with the case. Kealy was. The *Sunday Independent* was not devoid of strategy – Veronica was on her way to file a replying affidavit when she was gunned down.

Kealy utterly denied the notion that promoting Veronica as one of the country's leading journalists was a crime. Prendiville's attitude was, in his view, a greater crime. 'You do no service to her memory by portraying her as some sort of naïve young woman who was exploited by the *Sunday Independent*. If this were true, why did you not write this when she was alive? You did not because you know Veronica

163

would have denounced it as the lie that it is.'

Phoenix published that letter in their August 1996 edition. Below was a reply from Prendiville. He argued that it showed a 'total abrogation of responsibility in every single aspect of the relationship between Veronica Guerin and her employers, the *Sunday Independent*'.

If Veronica had decided to go to another newspaper, he argued, then the same issues would have been of concern. That did nothing to absolve them from the responsibility of considering her safety. The more impetuous and determined to get a story she was, the greater the duty incumbent upon her employers to ensure her safety.

If it was Veronica's idea to 'out' criminals, someone more senior had to approve it; at which point, it became policy. A policy which, in the sequence of events, immediately preceded Veronica being shot dead.

Prendiville may have seemed like a voice crying in the wilderness. The *Sunday Independent* could point to *Phoenix*'s long-standing hostility to the newspaper and dismiss his attack on their treatment of Veronica as simply more of the same.

But Prendiville was not entirely alone. Someone else was about to raise their voice, someone much closer indeed to the dead journalist.

14

A BROTHER AGGRIEVED

'I don't look on her as a heroine. Bring her back tomorrow
and put another thousand kilos of drugs on the street and I
really have to say, I couldn't give a shit about the drugs; I'd
rather have my sister back.'

Jimmy Guerin

Nobody really knew much about Jimmy Guerin. He was
Veronica's brother; he had been photographed at her
removal, at her funeral, as her body was lowered into the
grave. He was family; not as important, not as meriting of
sympathy as Graham Turley, just a brother, just family.

And as family, for the first few weeks Jimmy played along.
No one spoke out of turn. If anyone felt anger, rightly or
wrongly, towards Veronica's employers, no one said so.
Jimmy admits to minor outbursts of rage in the days prior to
the funeral, but these were naturally put down to the extreme
stress of the circumstances, and were forgotten. The family
pulled together.

Then, on July 27 1996, exactly one month and one day
after Veronica was murdered, this letter appeared in *The Irish
Times*, written to the editor.

Anyone who knew Veronica knows that she was an
extremely courageous person who was 100 per cent committed to her work and her paper, and who showed this
commitment in everything she did. However, this courage
and commitment resulted in the death of a 37-year-old

165

mother who, during six short years, became recognised as being one of the best journalists in Ireland, not only in crime but in the many stories she covered.

Lessons must be learnt by publishers, and hopefully this will ensure that no journalist will ever again lose his/her life while pursuing a story. I feel that no story waiting to be told is worth this price.

Proprietors and editors must examine the dangers to which they are exposing staff members. It is ultimately their responsibility to ensure the safety of the people in their employ.

Veronica was in great danger for close on two years, and I believe that steps could have been taken to prevent her death. For instance, if a team, as opposed to an individual, was assigned to such dangerous work, then you would have to kill an entire team to kill a story, and I don't believe that even the amoral people who gunned down Veronica would be capable of that task.

Insistence that security personnel travel with staff would also help, and should be examined. But if all this fails, and you have a reporter who insists on working alone, then in future an editor must say NO. It is not worth the risk, as no story is worth the life of a reporter. It is editors who decide what appears in papers, and I would appeal that in future they consider not just circulation, but the much wider implications when running stories.

This letter was signed and written by Jimmy Guerin.

The initial reaction was one of a public averting of heads. This letter was not part of the plot. In the ongoing story of the fearless young reporter dying at the hands of members of the criminal underworld, no one had scripted these lines. No one had considered a sub-plot where the near-silent whispers about her recklessness and the newspaper's responsibilities suddenly burst into the central narrative. It took the *Sunday Independent* some time to respond. When they did, in a letter to *The Irish Times*, it came from David Palmer, the managing director of Independent Newspapers (Ireland) Limited.

Palmer began by depersonalising Veronica, by situating her in a group.

Campaigning journalists of Veronica Guerin's calibre are a rare breed. They investigate organised crime, they work in dangerous war zones, they report on the activities of repressive and dictatorial regimes all over the world. They do so because, as Veronica's editor, Aengus Fanning, said on RTE Radio's *This Week* on Sunday, they are imbued with a vocational zeal far beyond the ordinary.

Then Palmer cut to the chase, to the one message he wanted and needed to get across; that the *Sunday Independent* was not guilty.

Their work is dangerous. They do it voluntarily. No editor can force campaigning journalists of this stature to do something they don't want to do. Equally no editor can ensure a totally risk-free environment.

If campaigning journalism were to stop because of threats, intimidation, or risk, it would be the end of a free press as we know it, and it would only be a matter of time before democracies all over the world became no different in this respect from the Iron Curtain countries in the darkest days of Communism.

I know that Veronica's editors often discussed her safety with her, as did her family. One of her editors, Anne Harris, urged her several times to move out of crime investigation into the political team. *It was Veronica's choice to investigate organised crime and to work alone* [my italics].

After the shooting incident at her home early last year, she was given 24-hour Gardaí protection for a time, but for obvious reasons she found it impossible to carry on her work under such circumstances, and requested that the protection should be lifted.

I agree with Aengus Fanning that Veronica would not have accepted restrictions placed on her where she felt they would prevent her from pursuing her investigative vocation successfully. Nor would she have accepted an order to stop her work.

The entire country is devastated by Veronica's murder, nobody more so than her family. We in Independent Newspapers share that pain and grief.

It is obvious that hindsight provides perfect vision and that, not withstanding threats and intimidation, nobody could have known that this awful and outrageous murder would happen. But if editors and journalists are to give in to intimidation, freedom of speech will be the very first casualty.

It was a remarkably high-minded letter. Similarly noble sentiments from the editor of *The Sarajevan* in mid-civil war, or the editor of an apartheid era anti-government daily in South Africa, or indeed a letter from any editor of a newspaper dedicated to campaigning journalism, might have had validity. But this letter was coming from the MD of a newspaper group, one of whose editors considered that calling the deputy prime minister of the country a 'bollocks' was a journalistic triumph.

Palmer spoke about hindsight, about no one knowing that Veronica would be murdered. He used the phrase 'notwithstanding threats and intimidation'. Palmer neglected to mention that the 'intimidation' had taken the form of gun attacks on her home and on her person, threats to the life of her child, plus a recent physical assault by John Gilligan. The *Sunday Independent* had itself claimed, after her death, that the second shooting – when she was wounded in the leg – was meant to kill her.

In September 1996, *Sunday Independent* journalist, Stephen Dodd wrote: 'It is now believed the first gun attack on Veronica Guerin may well have been a genuine attempt to kill her.' Dodd then quoted a Garda source who stated: 'Veronica always maintained the gun was fired at her head, and that it misfired. There were two attempts made to fire.'

So Palmer was wrong; people *did* know that Veronica could be shot dead; Veronica, according to the *Sunday*

Independent itself, knew it at the time of the first shooting at her person. Did her editors also know this?

Jimmy Guerin gave a few interviews with a reluctant media after his letter appeared. An interview with *The Irish Times* was never published, although some of the issues he raised were put to David Palmer a short time later, to which the now standard replies were given.

The Independent group, for obvious reasons, ignored the controversy. Its dominant position in Irish newspaper publishing ensured that the issue was never going to be given the wider airing that Jimmy Guerin wanted.

The Independent stable included either outright or part-ownership of the broadsheet *Irish Independent*; the tabloid *Daily Star*; the only national evening newspaper, the tabloid *Evening Herald*; the *Sunday Tribune*; the tabloid *Sunday World* and of course the *Sunday Independent*. The group also owns numerous provincial titles.

There were other reasons for the lack of appetite in pursuing the arguments that Jimmy's letter had prompted. In media circles it became known very quickly that Graham Turley did not support the publication of the letter; later it became known to Jimmy Guerin intimates in the media and elsewhere that the two men had fallen out for this and other reasons. Most journalists, involved or not, were disturbed by this bitter twist to the aftermath of Veronica's death, and few had the stomach to get embroiled in it.

Foreign journalists who came to cover the story swiftly saw that there were two camps: broadly speaking, the Jimmy Guerin/*Phoenix* camp, and the Graham Turley/Independent camp. The Turley camp did not welcome requests for interviews from journalists who also intended to speak to the 'other side'. The *Sunday Independent* had become the conduit for interviews with Graham Turley; requests were filtered first through news editor Willie Kealy.

Each side spread rumours about the other; Graham Turley, it was alleged, was completely under Independent control; Jimmy Guerin, it was counter-alleged, had some unstated agenda of his own.

Jimmy himself had supporters and opponents in almost equal measure. Like his sister, he is charming, clever, street-smart, but like her, too, he knew what buttons to push on the reporters who came seeking information and interviews. At times, to this author, he did seem to have an agenda and it was difficult to know what it was. Interviews were half-promised, then promised, then not delivered until one day, one year after his sister had died, Jimmy Guerin came to my house, charmed my children, smoked loads of cigarettes, cried for the first time ever in all the times we had met and told me his story.

Before he had sent the July letter, Jimmy told me he had met with *Independent* executives.

The funeral was on the Saturday, then on the Wednesday I went in and had my first head-to-head with the *Independent*. Earlier I had heard that the *Sunday Independent* was proposing to do an interview with my mother[1] that Friday, Veronica's birthday. Aengus had told my mother that if Veronica was here, she'd be out doing it herself. So that was my first, I suppose, major run-in with them. I drove in, in a fit of rage from my mother's house at a quarter to one.

I parked the car outside Independent House at about five to one and I went for a walk, because I just knew that I wasn't in the right frame of mind.

I cooled down and I went in at about three and I told them that I didn't want them doing the interview with my mother.

I talked to Willie. In fairness to Aengus, he did ask me to come in and sit down and talk to him about it, but I just fucking detest the man, so I didn't sit down. I went through it with Willie, and he gave me an assurance that he'd talk to Aengus. I told him I'd wait and I sat in the canteen in the

---

1 Jimmy and Veronica's mother, Mrs Bernadette Guerin, has told the author that she was not asked for an interview by the *Sunday Independent* 'per se'.

Independent and he came back five or six minutes later and said, 'Yeah, we have a misunderstanding but it won't go ahead.'

But they did it anyway, with Graham. They ran a four-page thing with Graham in the Living and Leisure section. 'Birthday without Veronica', or some fucking thing. Then the following Tuesday, Jim Milton rang and he offered me a holiday.

He'd rung my mother and she'd said, 'Talk to Jimmy.' Up to this I had been quite close with all my family. I was far closer to each one individually than any other member. I was always the bearer of the good news or the bad news.

So Milton rang and said that Tony O'Reilly would like us all to have a holiday and he would make Cork available with staff and food.[2]

The Guerin family discussed the offer, but declined it. 'Then he came and offered us things further afield, and I suppose as it got more exotic, it got more tempting.'

This was Jimmy's sole contact with the Independent Group until he wrote the letter to *The Irish Times*. The reaction, he says, was extreme. 'Jim Milton then contacted my mother, my brother and Marie-Therese – they wanted a letter from the family endorsing the *Independent*'s position and they didn't get it that time. They got it later though.'

That Christmas, Jimmy had no contact with his family, except for his mother; then, in an attempt to bring the matter to a close, he wrote a four-page letter to Aengus Fanning.

Strictly private and confidential – and more or less saying, you and I don't agree, but there are points which I feel I'm entitled to get a response to, which have to be addressed.

2 Tony O'Reilly's holiday home in Glandore, Co. Cork.

Such as, why did they have a fund for Cathal?[3] This caused endless pain to my family; it embarrassed my mother. Then there was Traynor's affidavit about Veronica, which they didn't reply to. It was a whole load of things and it was addressed cc Tony O'Reilly.

Two weeks later, a hand-written reply: 'Got your letter, nothing to add, Aengus.' I knew this was a case of – fuck off, don't be annoying us. I took it personally. And then I made the inquest statement.

At Veronica's inquest in the spring of 1997, Jimmy's solicitor read out a letter on his behalf, in which he again criticised the *Sunday Independent* for what he saw as its failure to take adequate care of his sister. Within a short time, a letter was released by his siblings, repudiating his comments. His mother had not been party to this. The affair created a rift.

'You know if Aengus Fanning had walked in and said to my mother, "I should have stopped her, I'm sorry", I would never have written to *The Irish Times*, none of this would have started.'

Jimmy is adamant now that Veronica should have been told to stop, regardless of how she would have reacted.

'I don't for one moment believe that she wouldn't have taken another role, done something else, if they'd really forced her hand. She would have called it something else; she'd never have let on that she was giving in to intimidation, but she'd have stopped. 'You see, this gets right up my nose: the public talks about Veronica, this heroine, this wonderful person, this brilliant icon. To me she was my sister, and that's where it stops.'

Jimmy Guerin was the first non-media voice to question the

3 A short time after Veronica's death, the *Sunday Independent* opened a fund on Cathal's behalf, to which the public could contribute. The move came amid controversy as to whether Veronica's life had been insured by the company or not. In response to questions on this matter by reporters at the time, the *Sunday Independent* replied that this was a private matter between themselves and Graham Turley.

responsibility of the *Sunday Independent* in relation to the murder of his sister. In general, his efforts were met by media embarrassment – few outlets were willing enough or brave enough to run with the baton that Jimmy had presented.

I found Jimmy's analysis both plausible and moving. Many people did, but were afraid to state that publicly. The *Independent* hand feeds too many to risk its alienation.

But equally, there were people, many of whom I interviewed for this book, who did not attach any blame to the *Sunday Independent*, the common denominator being that they had worked with Veronica; they knew her capacity for risk-taking, her unreal hunger for stories, her willingness, in her own words 'to do anything and go anywhere for a story'.

15

WHITHER THE BLAME?

As far as Damien Kiberd, editor of the *Sunday Business Post*, is concerned, nothing short of locking her up could have stopped Veronica from doing what she did. 'What should have happened?' he asked me during our interview. 'Should every editor in Dublin have got together and decided *en masse* not to publish her stories? I don't think so.'

Vincent Browne, formerly of the *Sunday Tribune*, shares this view, even though he refused to give an interview for this book. He also knew exactly how Veronica worked, knew the risks she was prepared to take, and does not blame the *Sunday Independent* for failing to protect her.

Similarly, Rory Godson, who worked with her on both the *Sunday Tribune* and the *Sunday Independent*, told me that if 'fault' lies anywhere, it lies with Veronica.

Her relationship with Traynor exemplifies the mystery of Veronica: a talented, attractive woman with so much to live for, yet capable of taking too many risks. If she had wanted to shaft Traynor, she should have kept her Garda escort, stayed away from Traynor and then done it. But if you express dismay at what she did, you're seen as either offering an apologia for one or all criminals, or else you're unfairly attacking her.

In all the time that Godson worked on the *Sunday Independent*, he argued, there was never any sign of pressure on himself or Veronica to come up with stories.

174

'The paper treats people extraordinarily well and has huge resources. It did not need to squeeze the last drop out of us. Veronica was better off at the *Sunday Independent* than anywhere else. She improved enormously as a journalist there and most of the credit goes to Willie Kealy, whom she worked well with. For the *Indo*, making an investment in Veronica was worthwhile.'

The *Sunday Independent* defended its treatment of Veronica in similar terms. She did what she did, she was determined and if death threats and gun shot would not, could not and, did not deter her, then how could they? They stated on several occasions that if they had refused to publish her work, she would either have left the paper or quit journalism. It is, of course, impossible to surmise whether Veronica would have left the paper or journalism behind, or whether, if she had, she would still be alive.

Veronica's close friend Alan Byrne gave me the most balanced view of the affair. He believes that Veronica did not herself understand the risks she was taking. But at the same time those in charge, if not in control of her, had a duty to understand them on her behalf. Part of the role of an editor, he argues, is to maintain a perspective that his or her journalists, of necessity, cannot.

When Veronica was shot in the leg, Byrne urged her to turn to less dangerous aspects of journalism. 'I remember saying to her, "Look, go and write about football, go and write about gardening . . . but stop doing this, you don't have to do it."' Veronica admitted that this was a possibility open to her, that her employers had made that clear. But she refused to take it. 'The week after she was shot, I went to visit her at home, which was probably the first time I'd been to her house. I remember she was sort of hovering around on crutches and we were watching an interview on TV that she had given earlier.'

In spite of the fact that she had gone to Traynor's house as soon as she was released from hospital, the front Veronica presented to Byrne was nonchalant, if still determined.

That day she was more interested in hobbling across the

floor and showing me the pictures that she'd just framed of herself with Eric Cantona and various other Manchester United players that she'd taken in the players' lounge about three weeks earlier.

I don't think she ever thought Cathal was at risk. I think if she thought he was at risk, she definitely would have stopped, or would have taken steps to remove the risk, because she was absolutely mad about him.

I can't believe that she can have realised the extent to which she was at risk. Logically you would have thought that, had she realised, she would have done something about it. I don't think she can have realised for a moment the extent to which she was at risk.

It is possible, Byrne believes, that Veronica's closeness to figures in the underworld meant that she did not believe she could be at risk. She had possibly received assurances that she was safe. She may have, in her enthusiasm to get stories, over-estimated the validity of such assurances, and the power of the associates that made them.

Certainly, only two days before her murder, even after the assault on her person, Byrne describes her as being of a sunny disposition.

'I was supposed to see her the following evening [i.e. the day after she was killed]. I had spoken to her about two days beforehand. We had a long conversation on the Sunday evening, talking about the England–Spain game I'd been to, and she was teasing me about cheering for England.

'We talked about the European Championships and who would win. She was due to come to London to speak at a conference[1] and pick up an award and she was to ring me on the Thursday evening.'

But her brother, Jimmy Guerin, told me that the assault by Gilligan had shaken his sister considerably. Her husband reports this as being the first occasion on which she had broken down in front of him (see p. 123).

1 The conference was titled 'Dying for the Story'.

Byrne also told me that on the morning before she was shot in the leg, she seemed 'definitely anxious'. In a telephone conversation, she had told him that 'she thought somebody had dropped her in it . . . that she thought she was in danger'.

Opinions will always be subjective, but it does seem that Veronica's emotions disappeared as quickly as they appeared; as if she had a unique ability to suppress her feelings, to hide them, not just from those who were close to her, but from herself.

Veronica's pursuit of dangerous stories, Byrne argues, was partially a feature of her character – very much in keeping with the dare-devil child we encountered at the start of this book – but also, an integral part of the wider job any journalist performs.

You can say that she shouldn't have done what she was doing, she shouldn't have been exposing herself to those risks. As a reporter your instincts are to expose yourself to those risks, to take the risks to get the story. After that it's a question for those in authority or the newspapers to decide whether they're happy for those risks to be taken.

It wasn't really Veronica's call as to what she should and shouldn't have been doing. It was somebody else's call and it was somebody else's decision as to whether they were happy with the way she was operating.

A reporter is not best placed to make a judgement, because the closer you get to something, the harder you'll work on it.

Curiously, the people who have been most critical of the *Sunday Independent* are those who neither knew nor had ever come into professional contact with Veronica. But they were avid observers of the *Sunday Independent* and of its journalism, and who ultimately can tell the real truth? Those who were up close and saw only the trees? Or those who took a detached, panoramic view and gazed at the woods in all the complexity of their colours and shapes?

There can be no question of Veronica Guerin's value to the

Sunday Independent. It was highly successful newspaper before she joined it in 1994, outselling all its rivals and becoming part of the public discourse about Irish society. But it still had a tacky image, despite its success, and at this period had no great reputation for breaking news or for investigative features, although some of its journalists, notably Sam Smyth, were doing some excellent work. Its strength lay in its columns and in its features, and this is what was marketed.

But the editorial 'gap' rankled. And when Veronica was successfully wooed from the *Tribune*, the editorial executives were ecstatic. Fresh from her Casey scoop, Veronica was a prize acquisition. As the months went by, and Veronica began to break exclusive stories, the newspaper acquired its missing editorial link. It could no longer be accused of being a non-news paper, or providing only 'water-cooler news'. It was now at the cutting edge of a certain kind of crime reporting and the journalist involved would soon become an authoritative commentator on these issues on TV and radio.

Strong evidence suggests that this was Veronica's main attraction for the paper. Author and columnist Fintan O'Toole suggested to me that Veronica's investigative reporting was, of necessity, highly popular. 'It looked like she was finding things out and telling people what they didn't know and that's a good working definition of news. But it was also rooted in that sort of moral certainty that the paper liked.'

Dealing in crime, an area in which the key players were assumed to be 'bad', built upon a consensus of opinion. Hence such journalism formed an attractive mix of both commentary and reportage.

'It fed off a set of prejudices about what's really wrong with Ireland. You could say that what's really wrong with Ireland is crime and that it's a small group of people, conveniently from urban deprived backgrounds, who are the ones corrupting and destabilising our society.'

As a result, her journalism acquired the quality of 'hard-edged social realism', without ever really having to go into the issues it raised; issues in which the *Sunday Independent* did not show any interest.

'The only way that the *Sunday Independent* would ever write about social issues of poverty or unemployment or class . . . would be through an attack on somebody who had raised these problems.

It's important to stress that the *Sunday Independent* was a very good operation and it understood its own weaknesses. And one of them was the lack of breaking stories, investigative stuff and Veronica gave them that.'

Another element of Veronica's attraction was that the *Sunday Independent* advertised heavily on TV, a practice which necessarily demands strong lead stories. Personalising its writers, elevating them to celebrity status, is a simpler means of achieving the same goal. But, according to O'Toole, the *Sunday Independent* was aware that they needed strong, exclusive stories to truly benefit from their costly advertising strategy. 'And of course over time, you can weld the two elements together. You can say "our stories will be by Veronica Guerin", who is herself becoming a personality, and whom we can dramatise and whom we can sell, whose face people recognise . . . who's . . . on television and radio.'

Regardless of the paper's distress at Veronica's shooting, O'Toole emphasised, it is impossible to see how the *Sunday Independent* cannot have profited.

'That doesn't mean that they were not upset and that they didn't worry about her before it happened. It's just that if you have an operation which is fundamentally about dramatising journalists, what better dramatisation can you have than [being able to say] not only is your most famous journalist shot, but is shot in pursuit of your own newspaper's stories?'

Such events assisted the *Sunday Independent* in presenting itself as a key player in a drama, the 'embattled, brave, campaigning, pioneering newspaper which was out there, as they say, taking on "official Ireland", taking on all the established powers in Ireland'. With such an image to maintain, the fact that Veronica Guerin really did have enemies, really was involved in a highly dangerous 'battle', acted entirely in the paper's favour.

O'Toole accepts that it is pointless to argue retrospectively and complain that someone should have stopped Veronica. 'I don't think the cynicism went as far as actually saying "We don't care whether she lives or dies." I'm sure they cared, cared deeply as colleagues.'

But he does call 'disingenuous' the argument that Veronica, if called to task, would have left the paper, or left journalism altogether. 'First of all, where else is there to go other than the Independent Group in Ireland? She would have had to move to another newspaper within the Independent Group, in which case the same sanctions and the same concerns would have applied. Or she would have had to go somewhere else, and any other outlet would, I believe, have operated with the same concerns, *The Irish Times*, the *Sunday Business Post*.'

The notion that Veronica was something akin to a war correspondent was, O'Toole told me, entirely misplaced. 'War correspondents operate in packs and there are always at least more than two. There's always a number of them in any given circumstance, and every possible precaution is usually taken by any responsible media organisation to try to protect them, in so far as that can be done.'

Veronica was not revealing truths that would otherwise have been hidden. There was a choice made, in terms of the way her stories were presented and marketed. With Veronica at the centre. The fearless young woman reporter.

'It's Disneyworld,' O'Toole told me; 'it's a film happening before the film rights have been bought.' Those stories, as reported by someone tangential to the drama, by an unremarkable figure, would have been devoid of that highly saleable, 'mythic dimension'.

And hence Veronica's isolation. Hence the lack of control and guidance.

'In order to have that dimension', O'Toole said, 'it needed to be her on her own . . . if they didn't know that, then they're not the brilliant professionals who created the *Sunday Independent*.'

It does, as O'Toole indicates, stretch credibility to believe that the people who were able to create such a highly success-ful and marketable package, with so much weekly tension and conflict, had no understanding of the risks faced by its central 'character'. The fact that she was meeting dangerous men, men who used guns, nailed people to floors and approached her with iron bars, was the sub-text to many of her crime stories. Had she not been in that danger, they would not have been such arresting stories. 'It was as if there was a tease going on in relation to the whole story. The tease was very dark and strange, and also sexual . . . this woman out on her own.'

A more experienced journalist would, O'Toole told me, have never allowed herself to become so involved, an observation which merely highlights the tragedy of Veronica's death.

'A lot of people placed in that situation would walk away . . . a lot of people who are brave and committed will say this is a challenge to me as a person and as a journalist. Now somebody who's more experienced as a journalist might have said, "Look, I don't have so much to prove that I actually have to continue to see myself as some kind of crusader on whom the fight against crime in Ireland depends fundamen-tally and critically."'

So did Veronica become victim of her own publicity, even seeing herself as crucial to the fight against crime? O'Toole argued at one point that Veronica, as a woman in a male-dominated profession, would have twice as much to prove, twice as much reason not to back down, twice as much reason to throw herself into this central role. But, nevertheless, he feels that her personal characteristics are not at issue. 'She should never have been allowed to be in a situation where somebody was not stepping in and saying, "This is not a burden you have to bear. This is not a question of whether you, as a woman, are letting down women, letting down women in the media, letting down the people of Ireland, let-ting down the *Sunday Independent*."'

Veronica's behaviour after being shot in the leg merely

demonstrates to O'Toole that she was extremely traumatised. And because of that, she should not have been offered merely the option of taking a break from crime reporting. It should have been made mandatory.

'Anybody with an ounce of common sense in that sort of circumstance is going to say, "Well, actually, your judgement might be suspect. You might not be the best judge of the situation that you are in at the moment." That's not a criticism of journalism that's just simple, ordinary decency to tell someone in that situation that they need somebody else to help make decisions.'

O'Toole argues that the backlash against the *Sunday Independent* was tempered by the fact that most of Ireland sympathised with them, for the trauma they felt at the loss of Veronica.

'If you were the editor and you had made a misjudgement and somebody had died on the basis of it, I think people would say, "Jesus, lay off these people, they must be going through an awful time themselves." At the start, there was a collective sense that at some stage the people in the newspaper were going to deal with the issues raised by Veronica's death, and that it wasn't fair to start raising all those questions now, because they must be going through hell.'

O'Toole believes that, had the *Sunday Independent* subsequently made an admission of misjudgement or mismanagement, the matter might well be closed now. 'People would have accepted that it was a terribly tragic thing which shouldn't have happened, but that people make mistakes and that they now understand and have addressed them, and it won't happen again. But the *Sunday Independent* never accepted any responsibility, any guilt.'

Instead of apologies, or any attempts to understand what went wrong, Veronica's employers continued the spectacle.

When she died, they had this ad that came on with a picture of her and a caption about news being something that someone, somewhere, doesn't want printed. Her death gave them a moral authority that they had never had before, and they started using that in their advertising.

That may have looked like a memoriam card for Veronica but it was still an ad . . . a very conscious and deliberate attempt to make sure that the corporate identity of the *Sunday Independent* was going to be imagined by its public through the features of this brave young woman who was shot.

Curiously, one of the first things the *Sunday Independent* did when Veronica died was to attack its former contributor and now a regular on its weekly hit list, John Waters. In this instance Waters was completely blameless, his 'crime' in the eyes of columnist Eamon Dunphy was not to have written about Veronica Guerin in the first column he wrote after her death.

In fact there were simple logistical reasons as to why Waters hadn't written about her, but Dunphy's attack forced him to analyse the other issues raised by her murder and by the manner in which the *Sunday Independent* had dealt with its coverage of crime. He came to the conclusion, he told me, that the *Sunday Independent* had never understood the difference between 'the public interest and what the public was interested in'.

Veronica's journalism made criminals interesting, according to Waters, rather than saying or doing anything about crime. It portrayed crime's key players as enigmatic, unusual people, with curious nicknames, dark private lives and odd views on the world. But what function did it serve, other than to sell newspapers? 'I mean usually you're actually just publishing titillating information, but were any criminals put behind bars because of anything that was written?'

As far as Waters saw it, Veronica fulfilled exactly the same function as the columnists and gossipmongers of her paper – even if she took greater risks. And she was motivated, in essence, by the same concerns.

In order to keep their journalism sexy and the cheques coming in for one journalist, [the method] was to call Dick Spring a 'bollocks'. In Veronica's case, it was to go out and knock on more doors and get more attention for herself.

I think a lot of journalists have a problem where their work is over-exposed by newspapers, where they really have to push beyond their limit in order to keep it fresh. If you get a reputation for being hard on politicians, you have to keep doing it more and more. The same thing probably applied to Veronica in terms of crime.

Waters also notes that various bodies benefited from Veronica working in this tireless fashion. 'I'm actually quite surprised that [the Gardaí] themselves didn't intervene. Maybe the stuff she did suited them. Obviously someone like Veronica had a lot of Gardaí contacts, and they were giving her information, maybe something that they can't pursue themselves, that they can't bring to a conclusion. So in some instances you need to work through the media in order to achieve your aims.'

Like O'Toole, Waters feels that Veronica's reporting also filled a nagging chink in the *Independent*'s armour.

Veronica's reporting gave the *Sunday Independent* credibility. Veronica happened for them at a time when they were beginning to come under sustained scrutiny by other media and by the public.

People had a sense of nausea about the paper which was becoming acute. And Veronica came along and she legitimised the paper. Every week they had real journalism, so suddenly you couldn't attack it as much as before. You couldn't criticise it any more without saying, 'Well of course there's Veronica Guerin, who's doing a very good job.' I actually always felt quite angry at Veronica for doing that because she was a brilliant journalist.

I know that she hated the *Sunday Independent*, her friends told me and anyway I knew her, I knew she was quite different. She was a supporter of Fianna Fáil, she'd worked for Charlie Haughey. She also had a very complex view of the world, of right and wrong, which wasn't the *Indo*'s.

Even after her death, Waters argues, the *Sunday Independent* continued to benefit from the moral authority lent to the paper by Veronica's crusade. It was this that particularly disgusted him.

My column that week, which I had filed in advance, was actually about water pollution. It was all about water charges . . . how I think that they're actually legitimate. And then I thought, God, everybody will be writing about Veronica, but I couldn't think of anything to write about her other than clichés. I couldn't think of a single word to write about her at that point, so I decided to just leave it.

I was very shocked and saddened by what had happened. But I had these ambivalent feelings as well. I could see the *Indo* milking it. I could see people coming up to them and O'Reilly there with his PR man and Fanning crying on the radio almost – conveying this sense that they had been trying to eradicate the cancer in our society, and to me they *were* the cancer. The *Sunday Independent* is the cancer.

And then a strange thing happened to me. I went to bed on Saturday night, probably about ten days after she was killed, and at about five o'clock in the morning I woke up with a start . . . in a nightmare. And in the nightmare, a man had a gun pointed at my forehead and I was experiencing this sudden access to something which you can't imagine in real life. Now I understood exactly the fear she must have felt at the moment she was killed and it was absolutely terrifying.

I've never known terror and I was shaking. I got up and I wrote this article about her and about how great she must have been. You had to be to do what she did, to go through that, again and again. And I said that I had my differences with the *Sunday Independent* but this transcended all that.

When Waters went into the *Irish Times* to file his copy, someone alerted him to the piece written by Eamonn Dunphy in that day's *Sunday Independent*. In that piece, Waters was specifically attacked for having written about water pollution. It was implied that he did not care about Veronica's death.

That was the lowest point for me in terms of the *Sunday Independent*. I didn't believe that it was possible for anybody to stoop that low. That they'd use a dead woman, that they'd hide behind a dead woman in order to have a go at one of their enemies.

I didn't know what to do. For about half an hour I didn't know what to do. Having written the article now about Veronica, I felt that to publish it would seem as though I was responding to it. But then I said, no, I have to publish it, it's how I feel. I just let it go, I ignored Dunphy.

But the whole thing showed me what those people are capable of. It was worse than anything I'd seen them do before and they'd done some awful things, not just to me, but to other people.

As for that TV ad they ran about her after she died . . . everything is marketing to them. But they did have a huge wave of public sympathy at that point. It wasn't possible to make political noises about them and it's never been easy to do that.

Waters believes that, had she worked for another newspaper, Veronica Guerin would still be alive. 'They give you protection in the sense of your ego but not of your life. Other newspapers tend to do the opposite; they protect your life but they don't protect your ego.'

Had he been Veronica's editor, Waters told me, he would have behaved very differently. 'I would have said, "We cannot do this any more. I am not doing this any more. We are going to demand from the state that it does its job and we are going to make an issue of that, but we are not going to put you out there to risk your life because the state is incapable of doing what it should be doing."'

For O'Toole and Waters, then, two of Ireland's most thoughtful journalists, the issue of Veronica Guerin's personal motivation is a lesser point. She courted danger, but plenty of people do. Even if she saw herself as involved in a crusade against dangerous people, her journalism contributed nothing to their downfall. The issue was that the danger was a 'commodity', seized upon and marketed, both up to and after her death.

CONCLUSION

Any study of Veronica Guerin's life from her early twenties would have revealed an individual who was capable of extraordinary deceit in pursuit of what she wanted. But the stories from her days in Fianna Fáil didn't travel with her; her PR escapades didn't travel, and nor did the real story behind the Aer Rianta injunction at the *Sunday Business Post*. Reports of how she operated as a journalist emerged only after her death.

Veronica was a brilliant journalist, but her brilliance stemmed from a personality which lacked the normal controls of personal and professional behaviour. A woman who would dare to forge the signature of the chief executive of a semi-State company; a woman who would rifle through a senior politician's files; a woman who would lie about her professional qualifications in order to advance her career, would go to equally extraordinary lengths in pursuit of highly dangerous criminals.

Veronica Guerin never discriminated. To her there was no difference between doorstepping a politician and doorstepping an alleged murderer. To her there was no difference between taunting a businessman in order to secure a story and taunting an individual whom she herself claimed to believe had ordered two separate gun attacks on her home and on her person.

But more than anything else, any woman who would take her infant son on potentially dangerous assignments with her should have been fired, or at least put into work where her child was not at risk.

Veronica Guerin died because a murderous, dangerous criminal and his colleagues shouted stop first, instead of the people who were firstly in charge of her, and secondly benefiting enormously from the stories she wrote for them.

It is unclear how much the *Sunday Independent* knew about the 'real' Veronica. She was a remarkable individual, highly manipulative and charismatic and more than capable of getting her own way. She rarely, if ever, worked from the office, at whatever paper she worked on, and as there was no editorial forum in place at the *Sunday Independent* that could have supervised her work and her practices more thoroughly, she was able to operate largely free of the normal newspaper controls. It appears that the only reason for spiking any of her stories was the risk of libel.

The system has changed since Veronica died. Her successor, Liz Allen, has spoken of new safeguards; colleagues report that Allen finds it very difficult to work on certain stories because the *Sunday Independent* is now so alert to potential dangers.

In an article in the National Union of Journalists' magazine, *Journalist*, in January 1998, Allen described the back-up she had received from the paper as 'phenomenal. They let me work largely unhindered, and yet have made me realise that dealing with criminals must be approached in a different manner. The issue of Veronica having been pressurised into getting exclusives has been much discussed, and they usually succeed in persuading me not to do something risky instead of just going for it.'

Clearly the *Sunday Independent* has learnt lessons from the death of its reporter, even if it refuses to acknowledge this in public. The question that remains unanswered is why Veronica Guerin was allowed to operate in the manner in which she did, even after alleged attempts on her life and the most grotesque threats on her son.

The *Sunday Independent* was a careful employer in all other areas and conscious of the mutual responsibilities staff and management have in relation to safe work practices.

In April 1995, David Palmer signed an agreed set of Health

and Safety regulations which were subsequently circulated to all department heads, including the editors of all the group titles. The guidelines are concerned with environmental health. The Independent Group will no doubt argue that they have nothing to do with the conduct of reporters in their journalistic work. Yet the guidelines clearly indicate two key things; that Independent Newspapers are responsible for the safety and welfare of its employees; and that if those employees failed to comply with safety advice, then disciplinary action, up to and including dismissal, could be invoked.

Under the heading 'General Policy', the document reads: 'Employees are reminded that they have a legal duty under the Safety, Health and Welfare at Work Act, 1989 to take reasonable care for the health, safety and welfare of themselves and of other persons who may be affected by their acts or omissions at work . . .'

Under a further section marked 'Employee Co-operation', the document reads: 'Where advice or persuasion fail to achieve compliance with safety rules and systems of work, it is our policy to pursue the matter through the disciplinary procedure up to and including dismissal or summary dismissal where a breach so warrants.'

Veronica Guerin was attacked on three separate occasions before she was eventually murdered. By their own admission, her employers tried to persuade her either to move into a safer line of work or to allow herself to be protected by the Gardaí. She refused to comply. No disciplinary action was taken. On June 26 1996 she died in their employ.

Since Veronica's death, I have often wondered what former *Washington Post* editor Ben Bradlee might have made of it all. He sits on Tony O'Reilly's board, O'Reilly on Bradlee's.

Bradlee is a media icon, and has been ever since Watergate. Internationally, the *Washington Post* remains a symbol of journalistic excellence and integrity – the polar opposite of the *Sunday Independent*. What would Bradlee have done had Veronica Guerin been his employee? Would he have hired her, knowing her background? Would she have died on his watch?

In 1980, Bradlee and his colleagues were gravely embarrassed by the Janet Cooke affair. A young and talented black reporter, Cooke had won a Pulitzer Prize for a story about an eight-year-old heroin addict. The story was later found to be fictitious. Cooke was fired and Bradlee later discovered that much of the brilliant CV she had presented one year earlier was as questionable as *Jimmy's Story*, her article about the alleged eight-year-old heroin addict. She had lied about her academic qualifications. Cooke later said that the pressure to perform on the *Washington Post* forced her into doing what she did.

In his autobiography, Bradlee devoted a chapter to the affair, acknowledging a 'systems failure' that had allowed the affair to occur. He also provided instances where he had sacked people, to show that he was an editor who demanded high standards of integrity from his staff. One political reporter was fired for making up an innocuous quote from Robert Kennedy. Another was fired for lifting a few paragraphs from the writer J.D. Salinger in a feature story about Washington's suburbs; yet another for lifting material from a local historical society pamphlet.

Veronica was no plagiarist. But she broke other boundaries in the manner in which she conducted herself professionally, and it is highly unlikely that she would have lasted a month on the *Washington Post*. In addition, Bradlee would never have permitted her to assume the high profile position she did – one which gravely endangered her life.

When Bradlee was editor, he wrote a chapter on standards and ethics for the *Washington Post Deskbook on Style* – a manual of editorial conduct in every area of the newspaper's work. On 'The Reporter's Role', Bradlee wrote: 'Although it has become increasingly difficult for this newspaper and for the press generally to do since Watergate, reporters should make every effort to remain in the audience, to stay off the stage, to report history, not to make history.'

The *Sunday Independent* broke the Bradlee rule. Veronica Guerin refused to stay off the stage and, in her dying, she made history.